WASHOE COUNTY LIBRARY

3 1235 02974 4336

W9-CUA-275

FILIPINO IMMIGRATION

Jim Corrigan

THE CHANGING Face of North America:
IMMIGRATION SINCE 1965

FILIPINO IMMIGRATION

Jim Corrigan

MASON CREST PUBLISHERS
PHILADELPHIA

Produced by OTTN Publishing, Stockton, New Jersey

Mason Crest Publishers
370 Reed Road
Broomall, PA 19008
www.masoncrest.com

Copyright © 2004 by Mason Crest Publishers. All rights reserved.
Printed and bound in the Hashemite Kingdom of Jordan.

First printing

1 3 5 7 9 8 6 4 2

Library of Congress Cataloging-in-Publication Data

Corrigan, Jim.
 Filipino immigration / Jim Corrigan.
   p. cm. – (The changing face of America)
Summary: An overview of immigration from the Philippines to the United States and Canada since the 1960s, when
immigration laws were changed to permit greater numbers of people to enter these countries.
Includes bibliographical references and index.
 ISBN 1-59084-684-2
1. Filipino Americans–History–20th century–Juvenile literature. 2. Filipinos–Canada–History–20th century–Juvenile
literature. 3. Immigrants–United States–History–20th century–Juvenile literature. 4. Immigrants–Canada–History–
20th century–Juvenile literature. 5. Philippines–Emigration and immigration–History–20th century–Juvenile
literature. 6. United States–Emigration and immigration–History–20th century–Juvenile literature. 7. Canada–
Emigration and immigration–History–20th century–Juvenile literature. [1. Filipino Americans–History–20th century.
2. Filipinos–Canada–History–20th century. 3. Immigrants–United States–History–20th century. 4. Immigrants–
Canada–History–20th century. 5. Philippines–Emigration and immigration–History–20th century. 6. United States–
Emigration and immigration–History. 7. Canada–Emigration and immigration–History–20th
century.] I. Title. II. Changing face of North America.
 E184.F4C675 2004
 304.8'730599—dc22
                                                                                                    2003013261

THE Face of North America:
IMMIGRATION SINCE 1965

CONTENTS

INTRODUCTION

THE CHANGING FACE OF AMERICA

By Senator Edward M. Kennedy

America is proud of its heritage and history as a nation of immigrants, and my own family is an example. All eight of my great-grandparents were immigrants who left Ireland a century and a half ago, when that land was devastated by the massive famine caused by the potato blight. When I was a young boy, my grandfather used to take me down to the docks in Boston and regale me with stories about the Great Famine and the waves of Irish immigrants who came to America seeking a better life. He talked of how the Irish left their marks in Boston and across the nation, enduring many hardships and harsh discrimination, but also building the railroads, digging the canals, settling the West, and filling the factories of a growing America. According to one well-known saying of the time, "under every railroad tie, an Irishman is buried."

America was the promised land for them, as it has been for so many other immigrants who have found shelter, hope, opportunity, and freedom. Immigrants have always been an indispensable part of our nation. They have contributed immensely to our communities, created new jobs and whole new industries, served in our armed forces, and helped make America the continuing land of promise that it is today.

The inspiring poem by Emma Lazarus, inscribed on the pedestal of the Statue of Liberty in New York Harbor, is America's welcome to all immigrants:

Give me your tired, your poor,
Your huddled masses yearning to breathe free,
The wretched refuse of your teeming shore,
Send these, the homeless, tempest-tossed, to me:
I lift my lamp beside the golden door.

The period since September 11, 2001, has been particularly challenging for immigrants. Since the horrifying terrorist attacks, there has been a resurgence of anti-immigrant attitudes and behavior. We all agree that our borders must be safe and secure. Yet, at the same time, we must safeguard the entry of the millions of persons who come to the United States legally each year as immigrants, visitors, scholars, students, and workers. The "golden door" must stay open. We must recognize that immigration is not the problem—terrorism is. We must identify and isolate the terrorists, and not isolate America.

One of my most important responsibilities in the Senate is the preservation of basic rights and basic fairness in the application of our immigration laws, so that new generations of immigrants in our own time and for all time will have the same opportunity that my great-grandparents had when they arrived in America.

Immigration is beneficial for the United States and for countries throughout the world. It is no coincidence that two hundred years ago, our nations' founders chose *E Pluribus Unum*—"out of many, one"—as America's motto. These words, chosen by Benjamin Franklin, John Adams, and Thomas Jefferson, refer to the ideal that separate colonies can be transformed into one united nation. Today, this ideal has come to apply to individuals as well. Our diversity is our strength. We are a nation of immigrants, and we always will be.

FOREWORD

THE CHANGING FACE OF THE UNITED STATES

Marian L. Smith, historian
U.S. Immigration and Naturalization Service

Americans commonly assume that immigration today is very different than immigration of the past. The immigrants themselves appear
to be unlike immigrants of earlier eras. Their language, their dress,
their food, and their ways seem strange. At times people fear too
many of these new immigrants will destroy the America they know.
But has anything really changed? Do new immigrants have any
different effect on America than old immigrants a century ago? Is the
American fear of too much immigration a new development? Do
immigrants really change America more than America changes the
immigrants? The very subject of immigration raises many questions.

In the United States, immigration is more than a chapter in a history book. It is a continuous thread that links the present moment to
the first settlers on North American shores. From the first colonists'
arrival until today, immigrants have been met by Americans who both
welcomed and feared them. Immigrant contributions were always
welcome—on the farm, in the fields, and in the factories. Welcoming
the poor, the persecuted, and the "huddled masses" became an
American principle. Beginning with the original Pilgrims' flight from
religious persecution in the 1600s, through the Irish migration to
escape starvation in the 1800s, to the relocation of Central
Americans seeking refuge from civil wars in the 1980s and 1990s, the
United States has considered itself a haven for the destitute and the
oppressed.

But there was also concern that immigrants would not adopt American ways, habits, or language. Too many immigrants might overwhelm America. If so, the dream of the Founding Fathers for United States government and society would be destroyed. For this reason, throughout American history some have argued that limiting or ending immigration is our patriotic duty. Benjamin Franklin feared there were so many German immigrants in Pennsylvania the Colonial Legislature would begin speaking German. "Progressive" leaders of the early 1900s feared that immigrants who could not read and understand the English language were not only exploited by "big business," but also served as the foundation for "machine politics" that undermined the U.S. Constitution. This theme continues today, usually voiced by those who bear no malice toward immigrants but who want to preserve American ideals.

Have immigrants changed? In colonial days, when most colonists were of English descent, they considered Germans, Swiss, and French immigrants as different. They were not "one of us" because they spoke a different language. Generations later, Americans of German or French descent viewed Polish, Italian, and Russian immigrants as strange. They were not "like us" because they had a different religion, or because they did not come from a tradition of constitutional government. Recently, Americans of Polish or Italian descent have seen Nicaraguan, Pakistani, or Vietnamese immigrants as too different to be included. It has long been said of American immigration that the latest ones to arrive usually want to close the door behind them.

It is important to remember that fear of individual immigrant groups seldom lasted, and always lessened. Benjamin Franklin's anxiety over German immigrants disappeared after those immigrants' sons and daughters helped the nation gain independence in the Revolutionary War. The Irish of the mid-1800s were among the most hated immigrants, but today we all wear green on St. Patrick's Day. While a century ago it was feared that Italian and other Catholic immigrants would vote as directed by the Pope, today that controversy is only a vague memory. Unfortunately, some ethnic groups continue their efforts to earn acceptance. The African

Americans' struggle continues, and some Asian Americans, whose families have been in America for generations, are the victims of current anti-immigrant sentiment.

Time changes both immigrants and America. Each wave of new immigrants, with their strange language and habits, eventually grows old and passes away. Their American-born children speak English. The immigrants' grandchildren are completely American. The strange foods of their ancestors—spaghetti, baklava, hummus, or tofu—become common in any American restaurant or grocery store. Much of what the immigrants brought to these shores is lost, principally their language. And what is gained becomes as American as St. Patrick's Day, Hanukkah, or Cinco de Mayo, and we forget that it was once something foreign.

Recent immigrants are all around us. They come from every corner of the earth to join in the American Dream. They will continue to help make the American Dream a reality, just as all the immigrants who came before them have done.

FOREWORD

THE CHANGING FACE OF CANADA

Peter A. Hammerschmidt
First Secretary, Permanent Mission of Canada to the United Nations

Throughout Canada's history, immigration has shaped and defined the very character of Canadian society. The migration of peoples from every part of the world into Canada has profoundly changed the way we look, speak, eat, and live. Through close and distant relatives who left their lands in search of a better life, all Canadians have links to immigrant pasts. We are a nation built by and of immigrants.

Two parallel forces have shaped the history of Canadian immigration. The enormous diversity of Canada's immigrant population is the most obvious. In the beginning came the enterprising settlers of the "New World," the French and English colonists. Soon after came the Scottish, Irish, and Northern and Central European farmers of the 1700s and 1800s. As the country expanded westward during the mid-1800s, migrant workers began arriving from China, Japan, and other Asian countries. And the turbulent twentieth century brought an even greater variety of immigrants to Canada, from the Caribbean, Africa, India, and Southeast Asia.

So while English- and French-Canadians are the largest ethnic groups in the country today, neither group alone represents a majority of the population. A large and vibrant multicultural mix makes up the rest, particularly in Canada's major cities. Toronto, Vancouver, and Montreal alone are home to people from over 200 ethnic groups!

Less obvious but equally important in the evolution of Canadian immigration has been hope. The promise of a better life lured Europeans and Americans seeking cheap (sometimes even free) farmland. Thousands of Scots and Irish arrived to escape grinding poverty and starvation. Others came for freedom, to escape religious and political persecution. Canada has long been a haven to the world's dispossessed and disenfranchised—Dutch and German farmers cast out for their religious beliefs, black slaves fleeing the United States, and political refugees of despotic regimes in Europe, Africa, Asia, and South America.

The two forces of diversity and hope, so central to Canada's past, also shaped the modern era of Canadian immigration. Following the Second World War, Canada drew heavily on these influences to forge trailblazing immigration initiatives.

The catalyst for change was the adoption of the Canadian Bill of Rights in 1960. Recognizing its growing diversity and Canadians' changing attitudes towards racism, the government passed a federal statute barring discrimination on the grounds of race, national origin, color, religion, or sex. Effectively rejecting the discriminatory elements in Canadian immigration policy, the Bill of Rights forced the introduction of a new policy in 1962. The focus of immigration abruptly switched from national origin to the individual's potential contribution to Canadian society. The door to Canada was now open to every corner of the world.

Welcoming those seeking new hopes in a new land has also been a feature of Canadian immigration in the modern era. The focus on economic immigration has increased along with Canada's steadily growing economy, but political immigration has also been encouraged. Since 1945, Canada has admitted tens of thousands of displaced persons, including Jewish Holocaust survivors, victims of Soviet crackdowns in Hungary and Czechoslovakia, and refugees from political upheaval in Uganda, Chile, and Vietnam.

Prior to 1978, however, these political refugees were admitted as an exception to normal immigration procedures. That year, Canada

revamped its refugee policy with a new Immigration Act that explicit-
ly affirmed Canada's commitment to the resettlement of refugees
from oppression. Today, the admission of refugees remains a central
part of Canadian immigration law and regulations.

Amendments to economic and political immigration policy
continued during the 1980s and 1990s, refining further the bold
steps taken during the modern era. Together, these initiatives have
turned Canada into one of the world's few truly multicultural states.

Unlike the process of assimilation into a "melting pot" of cultures,
immigrants to Canada are more likely to retain their cultural identity,
beliefs, and practices. This is the source of some of Canada's
greatest strengths as a society. And as a truly multicultural nation,
diversity is not seen as a threat to Canadian identity. Quite the
contrary—diversity *is* Canadian identity.

1 A TROUBLED PARADISE

For over a century, the people of North America and the Philippines have enjoyed a unique relationship. They forged ties after a turbulent beginning in which a U.S. victory in the Spanish-American War gave the country control of the Philippines. Throughout the 20th century and into the 21st century, Americans and Filipinos have engaged in business and trade, shared valuable resources, and fought battles alongside one another. The relationship between Filipinos and Canadians, though more recently established, has been just as fruitful.

Filipinos are the second-largest Asian group in North America. Filipino Americans rank behind Chinese Americans in population, and their numbers are growing. The 2000 U.S. Census revealed that there are just under 2.4 million people of Filipino origin residing in the United States. In 2001, the Republic of the Philippines was once again among the largest contributors of immigrants to Canada, with nearly 13,000 Filipino newcomers arriving on Canadian shores that year.

Despite their large numbers, Filipino Americans are frequently overlooked in discussions about minority ethnic groups. Smaller immigrant groups routinely receive a larger share of publicity and government attention. Some believe this almost makes Filipino Americans seem like an "invisible" segment of society. Filipino Americans have done little to challenge this, focusing instead on the immediate needs of friends and family.

◀ A fishing boat sits in the bay at the Philippine island resort of Boracay. Despite its natural beauty and international popularity with vacationers, the Philippines has been a troubled country from which many emigrants have left to start a new life in North America.

In the United States, as in their original homeland, they place far more importance on family and community affairs than on national politics.

Filipino Americans can boast a number of things about their former island home, located between Vietnam to the west and the South China Sea to the east. Warm, sparkling waters, sun-drenched beaches, and beautiful vistas have made the Philippines, which consists of more than 7,100 islands, a tourist destination that is still growing in popularity.

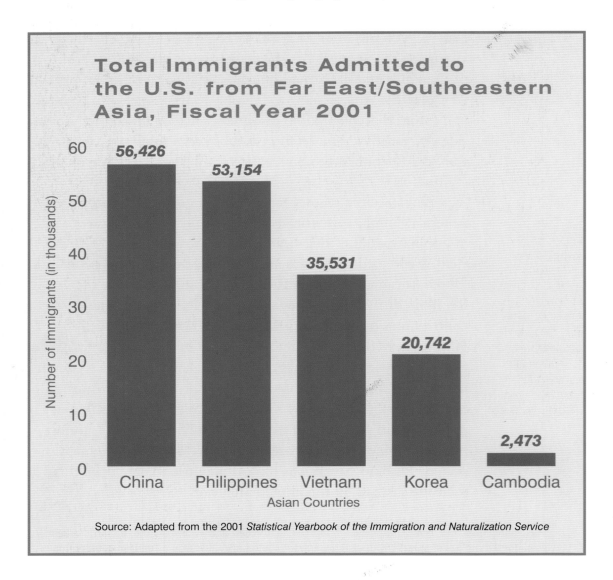

Total Immigrants Admitted to the U.S. from Far East/Southeastern Asia, Fiscal Year 2001

Source: Adapted from the 2001 *Statistical Yearbook of the Immigration and Naturalization Service*

Many Filipino immigrants continue to place great importance on family unity in their new countries. Extended families often pool their financial resources to satisfy the needs of family members.

Vacationers come from all over the world to sunbathe and frolic on island resorts such as Boracay and Cebu. Many of these islands remain unspoiled by civilization, and in some areas native tribes continue to live in harmony with nature, untouched by modern life, just as they did thousands of years ago. In many ways, the Philippines is a tropical paradise.

Filipinos in North America

Why would anyone wish to leave a place of such natural beauty and seek refuge in a foreign country? What makes so many Filipinos bid farewell to their friends and family? Sadly, the Philippines has been a troubled country. Extreme poverty, government corruption, and natural disasters are just a few of its many problems. Impoverished villages and towns lie on the outskirts of crime-ridden, overcrowded cities. As a result of these conditions, each year tens of thousands of Filipinos leave

their homeland in search of a better life.

In both the United States and Canada, Filipino immigrants have traditionally gravitated toward major cities on the West Coast. Los Angeles, San Francisco, and Vancouver are home to sizable Filipino populations. More recently, newcomers have settled in the Midwest and along the eastern seaboard as well, in cities like Chicago, New York, and Toronto. A significant number of Filipinos also live in rural areas, establishing communities in every state and province.

Fluency in English and an adaptive nature help Filipino immigrants assimilate into their new culture. But as might be expected, there are still hurdles that can stand in the way. Filipinos rely on one another and draw strength from their families to meet these challenges. Extended families live together and pool their financial resources. Friends and neighbors form social clubs for entertainment. Community leaders organize festivals and fundraisers to support these social clubs.

San Francisco is one of the major West Coast cities where Filipinos have settled in large numbers over the decades. In recent years, however, more Filipinos have migrated to regions further inland.

Social institutions and events not only strengthen bonds of friendship, they also promote cultural identity. Filipino Americans, like other immigrant groups, often feel caught between two cultures. Some customs and practices of their new home can clash with those of their native land. Nonetheless, by practicing some of the traditions and rituals they grew up with, Filipino immigrants are comforted by their past as they look to the future.

2 LIFE IN THE PHILIPPINES

The Republic of the Philippines is an archipelago, or group of islands, located in the tropical waters of the southwestern Pacific. Neighboring the Philippines are major nations such as China and Taiwan, Vietnam, Malaysia, and Indonesia. To the east is the Philippine Sea, and beyond that the vast expanses of the Pacific Ocean.

Although the Philippines consists of more than 7,100 islands, most of them are too small to be inhabited. Luzon and Mindanao are the two largest islands, with Luzon in the north and Mindanao in the south. The large group of islands that lie between Luzon and Mindanao are collectively referred to as the Visayas. Manila, the capital city, is situated on a large bay in central Luzon. The Philippines has a population of approximately 84 million; about 12 percent of those people live in or around Manila.

Inhabitants of the Philippines are known as Filipinos. They speak both English and the national language of Filipino, which is based on the various languages of the Philippines, including Tagalog, Spanish, and English. The vast majority of Filipinos are Catholic, but there are also some Protestants and Muslims. Residents of Manila and other cities work in shops, factories, business offices, and other jobs common to metropolitan areas. Those living in the rural regions are primarily farmers and fishermen.

This archipelago is no stranger to natural disaster. A lengthy

◄The green mountains of Luzon, the largest Philippine island and the home of Manila, the capital city. The Philippines consists of 7,100 islands, with a large segment of the Filipino population residing on Luzon and the second-largest island, Mindanao.

rainy season routinely produces flooding. Earthquakes, volcanic eruptions, and typhoons (Pacific hurricanes) are also common. Fortunately, Filipinos are an optimistic people and tend to take such setbacks in stride. This cultural attitude is summed up in the phrase *Bahala na*, "Leave it to God." Filipinos generally believe that problems eventually will work themselves out.

Culture and Values

Many Filipinos arrive in North America with little in the way of material possessions. Their meager savings have been spent on transportation, and they are hoping to start anew. They do, however, bring with them distinctive values and ideals. These principles help define who they are and shape who they will become as Filipino Americans.

Filipinos value family above all else. Concern for the family unit comes before an individual's own goals and self-identity. Being a good father or mother, a loving husband or wife, a respectful son or daughter, a dependable brother or sister— these are the things that matter most in life. Personal dreams and aspirations must be set aside if they are in conflict with the needs of the family.

Filipinos learn to have a strong sense of pride, striving to avoid *hiya*, or shame. *Hiya* is a guiding force behind much decision-making; it is an internal barometer that helps many Filipinos and Filipino Americans distinguish right from wrong. Many individuals try to avoid inappropriate behavior because of the shame it would bring upon them and their family. Filipino children tend to be serious about their studies, since failure to meet expectations would be a source of embarrassment, particularly given the strong value placed on education in the Filipino culture. Filipino adults display a strong work ethic, taking pride in their efforts to support their families.

Another important Filipino value is *amor-propio*, which can best be described as pride in one's self-image. *Amor-propio* is the strong face that Filipinos present to society. It is the light in which they wish to be seen by others. Filipinos also place a high value on hospitality, which includes providing a warm welcome and ample food to guests in their homes. This practice has been carried over into America.

Customs and Etiquette

The Filipino emphasis on family relations is evident in many customs. The godparent, often a relative, may play an integral part in a child's life well after baptism. In fact, parents may select godparents who they feel would be the best people to take care of the child should anything happen to the mother and father.

A debt of gratitude is known as *utang na loob* and it is taken seriously. Literally translated, *utang na loob* is "debt of the inner self." A Filipino who receives a gift or favor may feel morally obligated to not only reciprocate, but to provide the gift giver with something of even greater value. Foreign doctors and nurses on medical missions to rural areas often find themselves showered with gifts and souvenirs from the local population. More than just tokens of appreciation, these presents are intended as repayment for the medical services rendered.

Utang na loob has been known sometimes to set off a cycle of indebtedness, wherein both parties are locked into escalating gift exchanges. It is for this reason that in some cases Filipinos will turn down help that they need; they do not wish to become indebted to the person offering assistance. Interestingly, *utang na loob* helps ensure strong parent-child ties, since Filipino children feel that they can never adequately repay their parents for the greatest gift of all—the gift of life.

Filipino immigrants who return home are called *balikbayans*, which literally means "homecoming." They are expected to arrive with gifts for friends and family members, and they must be careful to visit these people in the proper order. *Balikbayans* are welcomed with much celebration, and jokingly teased about the foreign traits and mannerisms they have adopted. Traveling back to the Philippines is too expensive for many immigrants, so they send packages stuffed with souvenirs and presents. This practice has become so popular in recent years that a number of American companies now specialize in the packing and shipping of "*balikbayan* boxes" to customers' relatives in the Philippines.

Social functions in the Philippines rarely begin on time, leading to the coining of the phrase "Filipino time." Late arrival at a social gathering is not a sign of arrogance or disorganization; it is intended to show patience and self-restraint. Likewise, the guest of honor at a Filipino birthday party will wait until all guests have arrived to open gifts. He or she is not unappreciative, but merely wishes to avoid any group comparison of the gifts, a situation that could lead to *hiya* for some of the gift givers.

Beauty and attractiveness influence life in the Philippines, from business and politics to entertainment. Fair skin, pleasant features, and stylish dress are admired. An attractive person is expected to be charismatic, not to the point of appearing vain.

Many Filipinos have a strong fascination with American culture. American movie stars, professional athletes, and pop-music performers enjoy widespread popularity in the Philippines. Much like their American counterparts, most Filipinos may be more familiar with the latest Hollywood celebrities than they are with current leaders of their government. New York fashion trends quickly find their way to Manila, as do most American pop culture fads and crazes.

Early Filipino History

An appreciation of modern Filipino life can only be obtained through an understanding of the nation's troubled past. Filipino history is a tragic but fascinating tale of adversity and invasion. Despite the historical presence of foreign aggressors, it would be unfair to say that the Filipinos were ever conquered. These highly adaptive people instead learned to merge the invaders' customs with their own. As a result, modern Filipino society is a unique blend of native and foreign cultures.

The first people to arrive on the archipelago some 35,000 years ago arrived from Malaysia, traversing land bridges connecting the peninsula to the islands. (These bridges have long since been claimed by the Pacific.) The people did not settle in large groups, but rather as families, which over time evolved into independent tribes. Members of these tribes depended on one another for survival, which helps explain the deep devotion to family rooted in Filipino culture today.

Filipino natives killed Portuguese explorer Ferdinand Magellan during a battle in 1521. Magellan and his crew arrived to the Philippines searching for a trade route through the Orient and to convert the islanders to Christianity.

Arab merchants were the first visitors to the islands, followed by Chinese merchants. They traded with the tribes for gold, pearls, and tortoiseshell. In the 14th century Muslim missionaries arrived to the southern islands, instructing the native tribes in the ways of Islam. This religion took hold in and around Mindanao in the south, where over 4 million people practice Islam today.

In 1521, the famous Portuguese explorer Ferdinand Magellan arrived from Spain on an expedition funded by King Charles I. Magellan and his Spanish backers sought new trade routes through the Orient. During the voyage, Magellan and his crew often stopped to make Catholic converts of those they encountered, but they met their match in the Philippines.

After entangling themselves in a bitter feud between rival tribes, Magellan and 250 of his men were killed. The survivors returned to Spain.

Undaunted, the Spanish returned several years later and named the islands after the son of King Charles I, Philip, who later succeeded his father to the throne and became King Philip II. Early conquistadors used brutal methods, killing natives and burning their villages. Some Filipinos fled in terror; others fought back. When word of the atrocities reached Spain, King Philip II ordered a halt to the violence and sent Catholic friars to make peace with the Filipinos and convert them through a less callous approach.

José Rizal: National Hero

Born on June 19, 1861, in a small village south of Manila, José Rizal demonstrated a thirst for knowledge from a very young age. His affluent parents owned one of the few private libraries in the archipelago at that time, and young Rizal constantly had his nose in books. Finishing college in Manila, Rizal then traveled to Spain for training to become an eye surgeon. He socialized in Madrid with other Filipino students and quickly became a leader in the movement for Philippine independence.

Rizal wrote novels about the inequalities of Spanish rule in his native land, for which he was declared a heretic by Spanish clergy and exiled to a remote area of Mindanao. There he labored to improve the lives of his fellow Filipinos, opening a hospital, establishing a school, and devising better fishing methods. He also painted, wrote poetry, and carved sculpture. When a secret group planning armed rebellion begged Rizal to join them, he declined. Regardless, after the coup was put down, Rizal was implicated, taken to Manila, and executed. He was only 35 years old.

It is difficult to overstate the respect that Filipinos feel for José Rizal. He represents virtues—such as wisdom, compassion, selflessness, and courage—that Filipinos cherish. His image can be found in many places, from coins and postage stamps to the walls of classrooms and living rooms. It is likely that nearly every city, town, and village in the Philippines has a Rizal Street, and the anniversaries of his birth and death are major holidays for Filipinos living in the country and around the world.

With the exception of the Muslims in the south, Filipinos embraced Catholicism, gradually incorporating some of their own rituals into the faith. Friars gathered the far-flung tribes into villages, each with a church at its center. Schools, printing presses, and libraries were also built, but Filipinos did not benefit from them. The friars, wishing to maintain absolute authority over their flocks, generally refused to educate the people or do anything else that might improve Filipino lives. The friars used nonviolent methods, but like the conquistadors, are said to have craved power and wealth. Today, a Filipino who is lazy or only interested in personal comfort is disparagingly called a friar.

Spain established the first major settlement

In 1565, King Philip II of Spain (1527–98) sent conquistadors to the Philippine Islands to subjugate the natives and claim the islands, which were then named after the king.

in 1565 and ruled the Philippines for over three centuries, shipping the archipelago's resources back to Europe one ship at a time. The occasional revolt by oppressed Filipinos was always viciously crushed. Living conditions steadily deteriorated.

Fighting the Spanish and the Americans

During the 19th century, some young Filipinos from relatively wealthy families were sent to Europe for a modern education. When they returned, they brought with them ideas of freedom and national independence. These concepts spread among the towns and villages, creating a strong resentment of Spanish rule. For the first time, people began viewing their collection of islands as a country. They now thought of themselves as more than just members of a tribe or family, but also as citizens of a Philippine nation.

In 1872, the first major uprising took hold in Luzon. The Spanish once again responded with violence, this time executing three Filipino priests who supported the revolt. But rather than instilling fear as the Spanish intended, the priests' murders only provoked further unrest. A young Filipino doctor named José Rizal began publishing books and magazines calling for Philippine autonomy from Spain. Although Rizal encouraged only peaceful protest, he was accused of inciting revolt and was executed in 1896. José Rizal became a national hero and a martyr for Philippine independence.

Following Rizal's death, civil resistance rapidly turned into armed revolution. Spanish authorities could not put this revolt down because Spain faced another major distraction at this time—it was at war with the United States. On May 1, 1898, American naval ships led by Commodore George Dewey sailed into Manila Harbor, destroying the Spanish forces there. After the Spanish-American War ended a few months later, Spain ceded the Philippines to the United States for $20 million.

Spain's hold over the Philippines had ended, but a period of U.S. control was just beginning. Filipinos who assumed they had achieved independence soon realized that they were mistaken. Guerilla warfare against the U.S. colonial government ensued and lasted for six years, resulting in over 200,000 Filipino deaths. Most of the fighting ceased by 1905, except in the south where Muslim rebels continued to rebel. Although the U.S. troops were victorious, they had learned to respect the Filipinos' courage and tenacity.

In the decades following the suppression of the revolts, the United States set about reshaping the Philippines, introducing capitalism and a democratic-style government. A public school system was established, and Filipino college students came to America to study, some under scholarships awarded by the U.S. government. Filipinos embraced American popular culture and consumer products.

American interest in the Philippines was primarily for economic reasons—the islands contained an abundance of natural resources and labor. Major corporations opened subsidiaries, buying up land in and around Manila. Filipino laborers gained opportunities to migrate to the United States to work on sugar plantations, in fish canneries, and in other job fields.

Independence and the Second World War

The Tydings-McDuffie Independence Act, passed in 1934, laid out the plan for the Philippines' independence, and a year later, the Philippine Commonwealth was established. Another plan was set in place for the Philippines' gradual separation from the United States over the next 10 years.

The outbreak of World War II interrupted the independence plan, however. Japanese planes bombed American forces in Luzon the day after the Pearl Harbor attack on December 7, 1941. Imperial soldiers invaded shortly thereafter, forcing the ill-prepared American and Filipino troops out of Manila. Led by General Douglas MacArthur, the Americans and Filipinos regrouped and set up defenses along the Bataan Peninsula and Corregidor Island at the mouth of Manila Bay.

For four months, the outnumbered American and Filipino troops held their ground until illness and starvation finally forced their surrender. General MacArthur, having been rushed to Australia to avoid capture, promised his men and the Filipino people that he would return. Japanese captors forced the 76,000 Filipino and American soldiers left behind on Bataan to march up the peninsula, in formation, in what came to be known as the Bataan Death March. Over 10 agonizing

U.S. General Douglas Macarthur wades ashore with a landing party at the Philippine island of Leyte in October 1944. The U.S. military fought alongside Filipinos in one of the most difficult campaigns against the Japanese during World War II. The conflict remained undecided for four years until Japan surrendered in September 1945.

days, 10,000 men died from exhaustion and Japanese brutality.

General MacArthur kept his word, and in 1944 he returned to the Philippines with a massive American invasion force. Japanese troops refused to surrender, in many cases fighting to the last man in hand-to-hand combat. Skirmishes continued in the Philippines until Japan formally surrendered in September 1945.

Estimates of Filipinos killed during World War II approach one million. Manila was virtually destroyed. Thousands of Filipinos had served in the U.S. military, both in Europe and the Pacific, and, under special legislation, were subsequently granted American citizenship. Many more fought the Japanese occupation force as guerillas, and subsequently received payment from the U.S. government for their efforts.

In 1946, the Philippines finally attained independence. Although the Philippines was no longer officially an American colony, it maintained a close relationship with the United States. The U.S. government helped rebuild Manila and maintained a strong military presence on the islands. American businesses returned to invest in the Philippines, just as they had done before the war, and they found success throughout the 1950s and 1960s.

The Republic of the Philippines kept the American model of government, but it became infested with what is known as nepotism, the giving of prized government jobs to family and friends. While loyalty to friends and family can be a positive personal characteristic, using taxpayer money to reward close associates is a hallmark of corruption. This lack of public accountability can allow leaders to view the public treasury as a personal piggy bank, a situation, unfortunately, not unique to the Philippines.

The Marcos Regime and "People Power"

Favoritism and government corruption reached new depths under the Marcos administration. A World War II guerilla-turned-politician, Ferdinand Marcos ascended to the presidency in 1965. He and his wife, Imelda, wasted little time turning their newfound power into enormous personal fortunes for themselves and their friends. Shamelessly ignoring the plight of the millions who had placed trust in him, Ferdinand Marcos used his elected office to support a lavish lifestyle. Meanwhile, Imelda Marcos traveled the world famously wasting public money on shopping sprees.

With his term of office nearing an end, Marcos began scheming to remain in power indefinitely. In 1972, he exaggerated the threat of communist revolution and the state of national security to establish himself as dictator. Remaining traces of democracy were swept away as Marcos assumed total control. He declared martial law, amended the Philippine Constitution to help establish a dictatorship, and shut down all media except government-run newspapers and television stations. Human rights were disregarded, those with connections grew wealthier, and the Philippines plunged into debt. Poverty conditions remained, and those who did not live in poverty often feared speaking out about politics for fear of arrest or worse. Ironically, Marcos's repression and corruption likely helped communist rebels recruit more people willing to fight the government.

The assassination of Senator Benigno Aquino may have marked the beginning of the end for the

During a presidency lasting over two decades, Ferdinand Marcos established a dictatorship, declared martial law, and led the country into greater poverty and national debt. Widespread protest finally led to his removal in 1986.

Mourners pay respects to the body of Filipino senator Benigno Aquino, who was assassinated at Manila Airport in August 1983. Following the tragedy, an opposition group, convinced that President Marcos was behind Aquino's murder, launched a movement that eventually ousted the president.

Marcos regime. After spending eight years in prison for criticizing Marcos, Senator Aquino traveled to the United States for open-heart surgery in 1980. Upon his return in 1983, he was gunned down at Manila Airport. People had little doubt about who was responsible for Aquino's murder, persuading some to make initial plans for a revolution.

The mounting public dissension—and pressure from the United States, which had supported Ferdinand Marcos for his anti-communist stance—prompted Marcos to hold an election in early 1986. His opponent was Corazon Aquino, the senator's widow, and Marcos believed he could handily defeat her. To ensure victory, however, he rigged the election.

When Marcos declared himself the winner, incredulous Filipinos staged widespread protests. Nearly a million Aquino supporters flooded Rizal Park in Manila, demanding Marcos's resignation. Pressure from the U.S. government and the demonstrations, which came to be known as "People Power," finally forced Marcos out of office. He fled to Hawaii and died three years later.

Corazon Aquino restored the democratic government, freed

Corazon Aquino, who became president of the Philippines in 1986, delivers a speech in Manila in March 1987. Despite her attempts to restore democracy and correct the errors made by Ferdinand Marcos, she had limited success implementing economic reform and stepped down when her term ended in 1992.

political prisoners, and reinstated presidential term limits. However, despite making some progress, she was unable to make many of the reforms needed to improve the economy and the political system. Her successor, Fidel Ramos, was a little more effective at implementing these changes. Joseph Estrada, a former movie actor, won the presidential election convincingly in 1998. Unfortunately, his regime became viewed as corrupt, and mass demonstrations and general public disapproval forced him out of office in January 2001.

The Philippines Today

A former economics professor named Gloria Macapagal-Arroyo replaced Estrada, vowing to make government accountability and economic development priorities again. President Arroyo had moderate success in tackling both of these problems in the initial years of her term. She immediately declared that her family would not take part in government business, and she stripped public officials of the many perks they had come to enjoy under previous administrations. Arroyo also worked to promote the Philippines among the international business community.

Unfortunately, government corruption and the volatile Philippine economy are only two of the nation's many troubles. However, it should be noted that economic growth and development has increased in the years since Marcos left office. Arroyo has been forced to deal with the insurgency that took root in the southern Philippines during the Marcos era. Poverty among the Muslim population in Mindanao and the surrounding islands has helped the rebel groups such as Abu Sayyaf and the Moro Islamic Liberation Front. Government forces and Muslim rebels have regularly clashed for some time. These rebel groups are not expected to take power, but they can hurt tourism, affect the business and investment climate, and spread terror.

There has been another consequence of the poor living conditions in the southern islands: Filipinos immigrating illegally (without documentation) to nearby countries, especially Malaysia. For decades, Muslim Filipinos have journeyed to the

Filipino protesters demand the resignation of President Joseph Estrada in November 2000. Estrada's term was marred by scandal, and after months of organized protests, he was removed in January 2001.

eastern tip of Malaysia in search of a better life. The migrants are a source of irritation between the two nations; Malaysian authorities periodically round up the refugees, which is usually followed by Philippine accusations that the authorities are abusing and mistreating them.

The September 2001 terrorist attacks on U.S. targets have led to renewed cooperation between the American and Philippine governments. The abduction and execution of Americans and Filipinos, routine car bombings, and links with the al-Qaeda terror network have resulted in U.S. military assistance to eradicate Abu Sayyaf and other Filipino terrorist groups.

Despite the insurgencies and security threats, Filipinos go about their everyday lives, tending to their work, their homes, and above all, their families. Popular sports include soccer, basketball, and, in some places, cockfighting. Filipinos relish a good celebration, so festivals, banquets, and carnivals abound everywhere, from the largest cities to the smallest villages.

Travel among the islands is accomplished primarily via ferries,

At a large rally in Manila in January 2001, thousands cheer after Gloria Macapagal-Arroyo is sworn in as president. Arroyo has enjoyed more success than any Philippine president in decades, although the country has been beset by slow economic growth and continual clashes between government forces and Muslim separatists in Mindanao.

which are fairly reliable but occasionally hazardous. On land, most people ride buses or *jeepneys*—colorful, elongated vehicles loosely modeled after the abandoned U.S. Army jeeps of World War II. In many ways, the *jeepney* is emblematic of the Filipino experience: an object of a foreign power that has been transformed into something uniquely Filipino.

Filipinos who leave their native land usually do so for educational or financial advancement, or to join family members who have left years before. The archipelago boasts a number of universities, but students with the opportunity to enroll overseas take advantage of it. Frequently, students find that the host country's relative prosperity makes the thought of returning home upon graduation less than desirable. Wages in the Philippines are much lower than in the United States or Canada. In fact, many Filipinos working abroad do so not for personal gain, but to support their families at home.

The *jeepney*, a colorful, elongated vehicle, is a popular form of transport in the Philippines. The U.S. Army jeep of World War II served as model for the design of the *jeepney*.

3 IMMIGRATING TO NORTH AMERICA

The history of Filipino immigration to the United States can be divided into three distinct periods: pre-World War II, post-World War II, and 1965 to the present. Prior to World War II, Filipino men traveled to Hawaii, Alaska, and the West Coast in search of work. They are commonly known as the Pinoy generation. After the war, a new wave of Filipinos arrived. Many of them were the wives of American servicemen who had served in the Philippines. The third wave arrived beginning in 1965, when U.S. immigration laws were changed, which, in practice, allowed the entry of greater numbers of professionals, including Filipinos. To place Filipino immigration in context, it helps to first take a look at the history of U.S. and Canadian immigration.

Immigration to the United States has been characterized by openness punctuated by periods of restriction. During the 17th, 18th, and 19th centuries, immigration was essentially open without restriction, and, at times, immigrants were even recruited to come to America. Between 1783 and 1820, approximately 250,000 immigrants arrived at U.S. shores. Between 1841 and 1860, more than 4 million immigrants came; most were from England, Ireland, and Germany.

Historically, race and ethnicity have played a role in legislation to restrict immigration. The Chinese Exclusion Act of 1882, which was not repealed until 1943, specifically prevented Chinese people from becoming U.S. citizens and did not

◀ In recognition of the Philippines' independence, President Franklin D. Roosevelt signs and approves the Philippine Constitution in July 1935. In gaining their long-awaited independence from the United States, Filipinos also lost their status as U.S. nationals, and until the passing of the 1965 Immigration and Nationality Act, were subject to tight immigration restrictions.

allow Chinese laborers to immigrate for the next decade. An agreement with Japan in the early 1900s prevented most Japanese immigration to the United States.

Until the 1920s, no numerical restrictions on immigration existed in the United States, although health restrictions applied. The only other significant restrictions came in 1917, when passing a literacy test became a requirement for immigrants. Presidents Cleveland, Taft, and Wilson had vetoed similar measures earlier. In addition, in 1917 a prohibition was added to the law against the immigration of people from Asia (defined as the Asiatic barred zone). While a few of these prohibitions were lifted during World War II, they were not repealed until 1952, and even then Asians were only allowed in under very small annual quotas.

U.S. Immigration Policy from World War I to 1965

During World War I, the federal government required that all travelers to the United States obtain a visa at a U.S. consulate or diplomatic post abroad. As former State Department consular affairs officer C. D. Scully points out, by making that requirement permanent Congress, by 1924, established the framework of temporary, or non-immigrant visas (for study, work, or travel), and immigrant visas (for permanent residence). That framework remains in place today.

After World War I, cultural intolerance and bizarre racial theories led to new immigration restrictions. The House Judiciary Committee employed a eugenics consultant, Dr. Harry N. Laughlin, who asserted that certain races were inferior. Another leader of the eugenics movement, Madison Grant, argued that Jews, Italians, and others were inferior because of their supposedly different skull size.

The Immigration Act of 1924, preceded by the Temporary Quota Act of 1921, set new numerical limits on immigration based on "national origin." Taking effect in 1929, the 1924 act set annual quotas on immigrants that were specifically designed to keep out southern Europeans, such as Italians and Greeks. Generally no more than 100 people of the proscribed nationalities were permitted to immigrate.

While the new law was rigid, the U.S. Department of State's restrictive interpretation directed consular officers overseas to be even stricter in their application of the "public charge" provision. (A public charge is someone unable to support himself or his family.) As author Laura Fermi wrote, "In response to the new cry for restriction at the beginning of the [Great Depression] . . . the consuls were to interpret very strictly the clause prohibiting admission of aliens 'likely to become public charges; and to deny the visa to an applicant who in their opinion might become a public charge at any time.'"

In the early 1900s, more than one million immigrants a year came to the United States. In 1930—the first year of the national-origin quotas—approximately 241,700 immigrants were admitted. But under the State Department's strict interpretations, only 23,068 immigrants entered during 1933, the smallest total since 1831. Later these restrictions prevented many Jews in Germany and elsewhere in Europe from escaping what would become the Holocaust. At the height of the Holocaust in 1943, the United States admitted fewer than 6,000 refugees.

The Displaced Persons Act of 1948, the nation's first refugee law, allowed many refugees from World War II to settle in the United States. The law put into place policy changes that had already seen immigration rise from 38,119 in 1945 to 108,721 in 1946 (and later to 249,187 in 1950). One-third of those admitted between 1948 and 1951 were Poles, with ethnic Germans forming the second-largest group.

The 1952 Immigration and Nationality Act is best known for its restrictions against those who supported communism or anarchy. However, the bill's other provisions were quite restrictive and were passed over the veto of President Truman. The 1952 act retained the national-origin quota system for the Eastern Hemisphere. The Western Hemisphere continued to operate without a quota and relied on other qualitative factors to limit immigration. Moreover, during that time, the Mexican bracero program, from 1942 to 1964, allowed millions of Mexican agricultural workers to work temporarily in the United States.

The 1952 act set aside half of each national quota to be divided among three preference categories for relatives of U.S. citizens and permanent residents. The other half went to aliens with high education or exceptional abilities. These quotas applied only to those from the Eastern Hemisphere.

A Halt to the National-Origin Quotas

The Immigration and Nationality Act of 1965 became a landmark in immigration legislation by specifically striking the racially based national-origin quotas. It removed the barriers to Asian immigration, which later led to opportunities to immigrate for many Filipinos, Chinese, Koreans, and others. The Western Hemisphere was designated a ceiling of 120,000 immigrants but without a preference system or per country limits. Modifications made in 1978 ultimately combined the Western

In 1965 President Lyndon Johnson signed into law the Immigration and Nationality Act, one of the most pivotal immigration laws of the last 50 years. The act opened up doors for thousands of Filipinos and other Asians immigrating to the United States.

and Eastern Hemispheres into one preference system and one ceiling of 290,000.

The 1965 act built on the existing system—without the national-origin quotas—and gave somewhat more priority to family relationships. It did not completely overturn the existing system but rather carried forward essentially intact the family immigration categories from the 1959 amendments to the Immigration and Nationality Act. Even though the text of the law prior to 1965 indicated that half of the immigration slots were reserved for skilled employment immigration, in practice, Immigration and Naturalization Service (INS) statistics show that 86 percent of the visas issued between 1952 and 1965 went for family immigration.

A number of significant pieces of legislation since 1980 have shaped the current U.S. immigration system. First, the Refugee Act of 1980 removed refugees from the annual world limit and established that the president would set the number of refugees who could be admitted each year after consultations with Congress.

Second, the 1986 Immigration Reform and Control Act (IRCA) introduced sanctions against employers who "knowingly" hired undocumented immigrants (those here illegally). It also provided amnesty for many undocumented immigrants.

Third, the Immigration Act of 1990 increased legal immigration by 40 percent. In particular, the act significantly increased the number of employment-based immigrants (to 140,000), while also boosting family immigration.

Fourth, the 1996 Illegal Immigration Reform and Immigrant Responsibility Act (IIRAIRA) significantly tightened rules that permitted undocumented immigrants to convert to legal status and made other changes that tightened immigration law in areas such as political asylum and deportation.

Fifth, in response to the September 11, 2001, terrorist attacks, the USA PATRIOT Act and the Enhanced Border Security and Visa Entry Reform Act tightened rules on the granting of visas to individuals from certain countries and enhanced the federal government's monitoring and detention authority over foreign nationals in the United States.

New U.S. Immigration Agencies

In a dramatic reorganization of the federal government, the Homeland Security Act of 2002 abolished the Immigration and Naturalization Service and transferred its immigration service and enforcement functions from the Department of Justice into a new Department of Homeland Security. The Customs Service, the Coast Guard, and parts of other agencies were also transferred into the new department.

The Department of Homeland Security, with regards to immi-

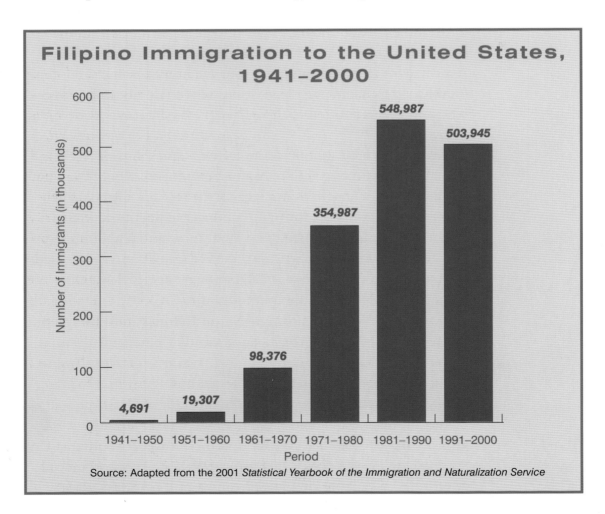

Filipino Immigration to the United States, 1941–2000

Source: Adapted from the 2001 *Statistical Yearbook of the Immigration and Naturalization Service*

gration, is organized as follows: The Bureau of Customs and Border Protection (BCBP) contains Customs and Immigration inspectors, who check the documents of travelers to the United States at air, sea, and land ports of entry; and Border Patrol agents, the uniformed agents who seek to prevent unlawful entry along the southern and northern border. The new Bureau of Immigration and Customs Enforcement (BICE) employs investigators, who attempt to find undocumented immigrants inside the United States, and Detention and Removal officers, who detain and seek to deport such individuals. The new Bureau of Citizenship and Immigration Services (BCIS) is where people go, or correspond with, to become U.S. citizens or obtain permission to work or extend their stay in the United States.

Following the terrorist attacks of September 11, 2001, the Department of Justice adopted several measures that did not require new legislation to be passed by Congress. Some of these measures created controversy and raised concerns about civil liberties. For example, FBI and INS agents detained for months more than 1,000 foreign nationals of Middle Eastern descent and refused to release the names of the individuals. It is alleged that the Department of Justice adopted tactics that discouraged the detainees from obtaining legal assistance. The Department of Justice also began requiring foreign nationals from primarily Muslim nations to be fingerprinted and questioned by immigration officers upon entry or if they have been living in the United States. Those involved in the September 11 attacks were not immigrants—people who become permanent residents with a right to stay in the United States—but holders of temporary visas, primarily visitor or tourist visas.

Today, the annual rate of legal immigration is lower than that at earlier periods in U.S. history. For example, from 1901 to 1910 approximately 10.4 immigrants per 1,000 U.S. residents came to the United States. Today, the annual rate is about 3.5 immigrants per 1,000 U.S. residents. While the percentage of foreign-born people in the U.S. population has risen above 11 percent, it remains lower than the 13 percent or higher that prevailed in the country from 1860 to 1930. Still, as has been the case previously in U.S. history, some people argue that even legal immigration should be lowered. These people maintain that immigrants take jobs native-born Americans could fill and that U.S. population growth, which immigration contributes to, harms the environment. In 1996 Congress voted against efforts to reduce legal immigration.

Most immigrants (800,000 to one million annually) enter the United States legally. But over the years the undocumented (illegal) portion of the population has increased to about 2.8 percent of the U.S. population—approximately 8 million people in all.

Today, the legal immigration system in the United States contains many rules, permitting only individuals who fit into certain categories to immigrate—and in many cases only after waiting anywhere from 1 to 10 years or more, depending on the demand in that category. The system, representing a compromise among family, employment, and human rights concerns, has the following elements:

> A U.S. citizen may sponsor for immigration a spouse, parent, sibling, or minor or adult child.

> A lawful permanent resident (green card holder) may sponsor only a spouse or child.

> A foreign national may immigrate if he or she gains an employer sponsor.

> An individual who can show that he or she has a "well-founded fear of persecution" may come to the country as a refugee—or be allowed to stay as an asylee (someone who receives asylum).

Beyond these categories, essentially the only other way to immigrate is to apply for and receive one of the "diversity" visas, which are granted annually by lottery to those from "underrepresented" countries.

In 1996 changes to the law prohibited nearly all incoming immigrants from being eligible for federal public benefits, such as welfare, during their first five years in the country. Refugees were mostly excluded from these changes. In addition, families who sponsor relatives must sign an affidavit of support showing they can financially take care of an immigrant who falls on hard times.

A Short History of Canadian Immigration

In the 1800s, immigration into Canada was largely unrestricted. Farmers and artisans from England and Ireland made up a significant portion of 19th-century immigrants. England's Parliament passed laws that facilitated and encouraged the voyage to North America, particularly for the poor.

After the United States barred Chinese railroad workers from settling in the country, Canada encouraged the immigration of Chinese laborers to assist in the building of Canadian railways. Responding to the racial views of the time, the Canadian Parliament began charging a "head tax" for Chinese and South Asian (Indian) immigrants in 1885. The fee of $50—later raised to $500—was well beyond the means of laborers making one or two dollars a day. Later, the government sought additional ways to prohibit Asians from entering the country. For example, it decided to require a "continuous journey," meaning that immigrants to Canada had to travel from their country on a boat that made an uninterrupted passage. For immigrants or asylum seekers from Asia this was nearly impossible.

As the 20th century progressed, concerns about race led to further restrictions on immigration to Canada. These restrictions particularly hurt Jewish and other refugees seeking to flee persecution in Europe. Government statistics indicate that Canada accepted no more than 5,000 Jewish refugees before and during the Holocaust.

After World War II, Canada, like the United States, began accepting thousands of Europeans displaced by the war. Canada's laws were modified to accept these war refugees, as well as Hungarians fleeing Communist authorities after the crushing of the 1956 Hungarian Revolution.

The Immigration Act of 1952 in Canada allowed for a "tap on, tap off" approach to immigration, granting administrative authorities the power to allow more immigrants into the country in good economic times, and fewer in times of recession. The shortcoming of such an approach is that there is little evidence immigrants harm a national economy and much evidence they contribute to economic growth, particularly in the growth of the labor force.

In 1966 the government of Prime Minister Lester Pearson introduced a policy statement stressing how immigrants were key to Canada's economic growth. With Canada's relatively small population base, it became clear that in the absence of newcomers, the country would not be able to grow. The policy was introduced four years after Parliament enacted important legislation that eliminated Canada's own version of racially based national-origin quotas.

In 1967 a new law established a points system that awarded entry to potential immigrants using criteria based primarily on an individual's age, language ability, skills, education, family relationships, and job prospects. The total points needed for entry of an immigrant is set by the Minister of Citizenship and Immigration Canada. The new law also established a category for humanitarian (refugee) entry.

The 1976 Immigration Act refined and expanded the possibility for entry under the points system, particularly for individuals seeking to sponsor family members. The act also expanded refugee and asylum law to comport with Canada's international obligations. The law established five basic categories for immigration into Canada: 1) family; 2) humanitarian; 3) independents (including skilled workers), who immigrate to Canada on their own; 4) assisted relatives; and 5) business immigrants (including investors, entrepreneurs, and the self-employed).

The new Immigration and Refugee Protection Act, which took effect June 28, 2002, made a series of modifications to existing Canadian immigration law. The act, and the regulations that followed, toughened rules on those seeking asylum and the process for removing people unlawfully in Canada.

The law modified the points system, adding greater flexibility for skilled immigrants and temporary workers to become permanent residents, and evaluating skilled workers on the weight of their transferable skills as well as those of their specific occupation. The legislation also made it easier for employers to have a labor shortage declared in an industry or sector, which would facilitate the entry of foreign workers in that industry or sector.

On family immigration, the act permitted parents to sponsor dependent children up to the age of 22 (previously 19 was the maximum age at which a child could be sponsored for immigration). The act also allowed partners in common-law arrangements, including same-sex partners, to be considered as family members for the purpose of immigration sponsorship.

In August 1898 U.S. soldiers take down the Spanish flag and prepare to hoist the American flag in its place, following victory at the Battle of Manila Bay during the Spanish-American War. Once the Philippines became a U.S. territory, Filipinos were thereafter considered U.S. nationals and, in the years up until Philippine independence, could easily move to the United States.

The Early Years of Filipino Immigration

Only anecdotal evidence exists of Filipinos living in North America during the early years of the 20th century. By 1920, they numbered approximately 5,600. At that same time, however, the U.S. territory of Hawaii was experiencing an influx of Filipinos. Hawaiian sugar growers needed labor and Filipino farmers came in droves, despite the horrid working conditions of the sugar plantations. Others journeyed northward to the salmon canneries of Alaska. Soon, Filipinos became key components of the workforce of both of these industries.

New arrivals from Hawaii, Alaska, and directly from the Philippines suddenly caused the Filipino presence in America to explode. By 1930 over 45,000 were residing in the United States, primarily on the West Coast. These immigrants were met with suspicion and prejudice, as were other Asian peoples

Filipino Doctors in America

Before practicing in the United States, foreign doctors must pass numerous examinations to prove that their skills meet American medical standards. Even after successfully completing this enormous battery of tests, some foreign physicians find that American colleagues still doubt their abilities. Such was the case for Edgar Gamboa, a Filipino surgeon who emigrated from Cebu in the Visayas. In Yen Le Espiritu's book *Filipino American Lives*, published in 1995, Gamboa described the resistance he first encountered upon arriving in America:

> It is a very difficult process for a foreign-born physician to establish himself in the medical profession here unless he is extremely determined. For instance, when I arrived in 1976, it was next to impossible to get into a decent surgical program. I could not even get past the door for an interview. . . . I would not categorize the situation as blatant discrimination. It is a more subtle form of racism, where people feel that an individual who does not carry the right genes, whose skin is a tad darker, or who comes from an unfamiliar university, somehow could not possibly be as qualified and talented and educated. If it is any consolation, I have noticed that as one goes higher in his or her career, discrimination diminishes proportionally. Now that I am an established surgeon, for instance, people accept me as a colleague, no longer as a mysterious foreign doctor.

during that time. Employment opportunities were limited to servile jobs, even for college-educated Filipinos. Ten states actually banned marriages between whites and "Mongolians" (an incorrect label for Filipinos). Beginning with California in 1913, several states also barred Asians, including Filipinos, from inheriting or owning property.

Filipinos were exempted from the 1924 national-origin quotas law, since residents of the Philippines were considered "nationals" of the United States, meaning that although they were not U.S. citizens, they had the right to enter America, whereas "aliens" did not.

The federal legislation that first authorized Philippine sovereignty in 1934 was a mixed blessing for Filipino Americans. It promised a long-awaited independence to their beloved islands, but at the same time it limited new Filipino immigrants to an incredibly low quota of only 50 per year. Accordingly, those already living in the United States were forced to abandon the dream of reuniting with their families. Though the Filipino Americans were crushed by the news, it is believed that most elected to remain in their new country. The federal government offered free passage for anyone wishing to return to the Philippines, but fewer than 2,200 accepted.

World War II brought many more Filipino immigrants to America, as exceptions were made to the quota system. Aside from those who earned U.S. citizenship through their military service, the Filipino brides of American servicemen were also eligible. These women known as "war brides" changed the demographic makeup of Filipino Americans. Prior to the war, most of the immigrants had been men, but now there were a significant number of Filipinas as well. No longer concentrated solely on the West Coast, Filipino families and families with mixed couples became a common and accepted part of communities around the country. The shared experience of having faced the same enemy during the war likely helped to diminish discrimination.

In recognition for the Filipinos' contributions to the war

effort, President Harry Truman signed the Filipino Naturalization Act in 1946, which allowed Filipinos to become U.S. citizens. That year, Congress passed a law to grant U.S. citizenship to Filipinos who entered America prior to March 24, 1934. With yet another piece of legislation, Congress raised the Filipino annual immigration quota to 100, which stayed in place until 1965. However, those Filipinos who lived continuously in America for three years prior to November 30, 1941, were allowed to sponsor a wife or minor child outside the quotas.

A severe shortage of American nurses opened the door for more Filipinas. The Information and Education Exchange Act, passed in 1948, also provided opportunities to Filipino nurses, through indirect means. The act, which permitted foreign nursing students to remain in the United States for two years after graduation, was intended to give foreign nurses an opportunity for further study and practical experience in American hospitals before returning to their native land. However, many hospitals found the English-speaking Filipinas an ideal remedy for the nursing shortfall and retained their services indefinitely. Soon the islands were exporting doctors as well, and Filipino students hoping to migrate to America entered medical school in increasing numbers.

By 1960, over 180,000 Filipinos were living in the United States, the new growth owing primarily to the influx of military families and health care workers. All other Filipinos were still limited by the annual quota first imposed in 1934. Although the immigration laws had subsequently been modified to raise the limit from 50 to 100, it hardly made a difference. Fortunately, for those who dreamed of a new life in America, immigration policy was about to shift dramatically within the next few years.

New U.S. Immigration Laws

The Immigration and Nationality Act of 1965 changed immigration to the United States for Filipinos as much as for any ethnic group, although the achievements of the early Filipinos in America were also significant to an improved system of immigration. Inroads previously made by Filipino doctors and nurses, combined with the characteristically Filipino devotion to keeping the family together, poised the Philippines to be a major contributor of immigrants to the United States.

The new "family-friendly" policy allowed immigration numbers to increase. A Filipino doctor given a professional preference was entitled to bring his wife and children to the United States. After several years, if the doctor's wife became a U.S. citizen, she then might be able to sponsor other family members for admission. In the decade following the 1965 act, some 230,000 Filipinos came to the United States. By 1980, the number of Philippine-born persons permanently residing in America totaled over half a million.

The increase in foreign doctors, particularly Filipino doctors, migrating to the United States caused the medical associations to seek protection from competition, even if there was little evidence of widespread unemployment among physicians in the United States. In 1976, they successfully lobbied to have "physician" removed from the list of preferential immigrant professions. The flow of Filipino doctors slowed to a trickle as a result, but nurses remained in strong demand, as they still do today. Some Filipino physicians responded by taking nursing jobs in order to gain entry, hoping to eventually become practicing doctors after they had arrived in the United States.

The Filipino American population continued to increase during the 1980s. By the close of that decade over 912,000 Philippine-born people lived in the United States, accounting for nearly half of all the immigrants hailing from Southeast Asia. This figure does not include the American-born children of these immigrants, who held U.S. citizenship but were raised in the Filipino tradition. Nor does it include Filipinos living illegally in America at that time. Today, approximately 2 percent of undocumented immigrants in the United States are from the Philippines.

Of the approximately 51,000 Filipinos admitted in the year

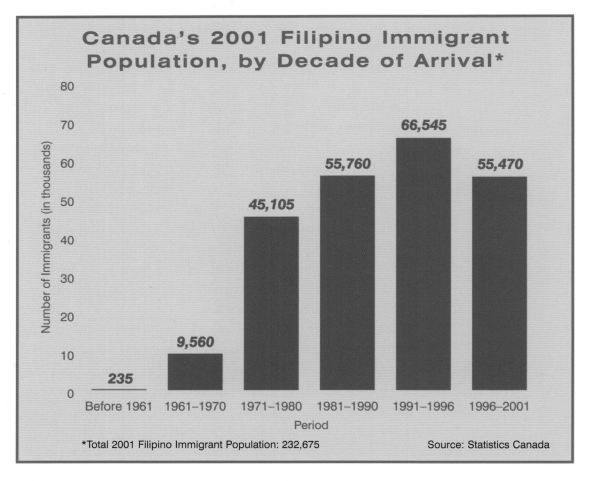

Canada's 2001 Filipino Immigrant Population, by Decade of Arrival*

Number of Immigrants (in thousands)

Period	Value
Before 1961	235
1961–1970	9,560
1971–1980	45,105
1981–1990	55,760
1991–1996	66,545
1996–2001	55,470

*Total 2001 Filipino Immigrant Population: 232,675   Source: Statistics Canada

2002, roughly 38,500 were related to a U.S. citizen and 12,500 were granted entry based on their profession. Today thousands of other Filipinos enter each year on a temporary basis, either as students or workers. Many apply for lawful permanent residence and go on to become naturalized U.S. citizens. In 2002, the total number of Filipino immigrants legally residing in the United States had increased to approximately 1.2 million.

The Immigration Act of 1990 addressed a key issue for many Filipinos. After World War II, all Filipinos who had served in the American military were deemed eligible for U.S. citizenship. However, that offer was not extended to veterans who had served in Philippine military units. For decades, these veterans and their supporters argued that they had been done an injustice. After fighting alongside American soldiers and serving in the armed forces of a U.S. possession, they too wanted recognition in the form of American citizenship.

Under Section 450 of the Immigration Act of 1990, these World War II veterans were finally declared eligible for citizenship. Many had not lived to see the day. Others were no longer interested in migrating, content to live out their final years on the islands they had so admirably defended. But some of these men, now grandfathers and great-grandfathers, traversed the Pacific in order to claim their U.S. citizenship.

Filipino Immigration to Canada

As in the case of Filipino immigration to the United States, Canada's free market and democratic-style government have been the primary attractions for Filipinos immigrants. Recent statistics for Canada tell a story of steady growth of Filipino immigration. Canadian officials anticipate that this pattern will continue well into the future.

Filipinos began arriving to Canada in significant numbers only a few decades ago. Before the 1960s, Filipinos and other Asian groups were discouraged by the "head tax" they had to pay. After immigration laws were changed, however, Canada began to welcome Asians as a source of economic and cultural enrichment, and the numbers of Filipino immigrants to the country increased significantly.

The changes to Canada's immigration laws altered the source-country totals of Canada's immigrants. Prior to the 1960s, newcomers to Canada primarily hailed from countries like the United Kingdom, Italy, Germany, the Netherlands, and Poland. But after the changes were implemented, the numbers of immigrants from countries such as China, India, and the Philippines began to grow. In 2001, the Philippines ranked fourth among countries of origin for immigrants to Canada; in 1961, it had not even been in the top 10. By mid-2002, roughly a quarter of a million Filipino immigrants resided in Canada.

4 THE FILIPINO AMERICAN LIFESTYLE

How do Filipinos make a living once they arrive in North America? Where do they choose to settle? What are their main interests and diversions? Of course, the answers to these questions are just as diverse as the group of Filipinos coming to North America, but it is possible to identify some trends and preferences. These tendencies provide insight into the Filipino American lifestyle.

In 2002, the U.S. Census Bureau released a profile of America's "Asian and Pacific Islander" population, of which Filipino Americans make up a sizable portion. In fact, of the 11.9 million people classified as Asian and Pacific Islanders, 2.4 million (20 percent) identified themselves as Filipino Americans. Only Chinese Americans had a greater population, with 2.7 million people.

The Census Bureau statistics revealed some interesting details about the lives of Asian Pacific Americans. Their median household income in the year 2000 was $55,525, an all-time high for this ethnic group. Forty-four percent of Asian Pacific adults age 25 and over held a bachelor's degree or higher, compared with an overall national average of 26 percent. Nearly half of all Asian Pacific Americans resided in the metropolitan areas of Los Angeles, New York, and San Francisco. In 1997, Asian Pacific Americans owned 913,000 businesses and employed more than 2.2 million people.

Other Census Bureau statistics showed that the median age

◀ Los Angeles remains one of the most popular North American cities to settle among Filipinos. In 2001, over 5,000 Filipinos who became naturalized were reported to reside in Los Angeles.

for Asian Pacific Americans was 31.1 in the year 2000, compared to 35.3 for the overall U.S. population. Married couples headed 80 percent of the nation's 2.5 million Asian and Pacific Islander families. The majority of households had a computer. Approximately 43 percent of Asian Pacific Americans who were eligible voted in the elections of 2000.

Again, these figures apply to all people originating from Asia and the Pacific Islands, and although Filipinos are well represented within that broad category, the data do not specifically pinpoint statistics concerning Filipino Americans.

Education and Employment

A top-quality education carries tremendous weight in the Philippines. It is considered to be among the greatest gifts that parents can bestow upon their children. When parents are unable to pay tuition bills by themselves, often the oldest child will forgo college and begin working so that younger siblings may enroll. Similar sacrifices are made in Filipino American households, with parents working countless hours of overtime so that their sons and daughters may maximize their educational opportunities.

The longstanding tradition of Filipino doctors and nurses immigrating to the United States is still evident in employment statistics today. The INS reported in the 2001 *Statistical Yearbook* that of the 13,346 Filipinos who reported their occupation type upon entering the United States in 2001, 48 percent were classified in the "professional specialty and technical" group, which includes health care

A Filipina sells produce in a street market. Many Filipino professionals who have immigrated to the United States initially find work as produce dealers, storeowners, or restaurant owners while working to meet requirements to practice their professions in the U.S.

Guide to Filipino Cuisine

The readily available ingredients of fish, rice, chicken, and pork dominate Filipino cooking. Culinary techniques of other cultures, particularly China and Spain, are apparent in most meals. *Sinigang*, a sour soup, is one of the few dishes with no discernible foreign influence. Though Filipino food may not enjoy the same popularity in the United States as the cuisine of other nations, Filipino restaurants can be found in cities with a strong Filipino American presence. Below is a sampling of the more popular dishes:

adobo—a stew of chicken and pork with vinegar and soy sauce.

bagoong—tiny shrimp fermented in salt.

bibingka—a dessert made of coconut cream, rice, and brown sugar.

halo-halo—mixed fruits in crushed ice and milk, served as dessert.

kare-kare—oxtail stew with pieces of tripe and vegetables in peanut sauce.

leche flan—egg custard with caramel topping.

lechon—a whole roasted pig served only on special occasions.

lumpia— Filipino egg rolls.

mechado—a stir-fry of beef and vegetables in tomato sauce.

pancit—noodles with vegetables, sausage, and shrimp.

rellenong manok—a whole chicken stuffed with a mixture of ground chicken, pork, and ham, plus sausages and hard-boiled eggs.

sinigang—a sour broth with pork, beef, or seafood and vegetables.

tinolang tahong—soup made with mussels steamed in ginger root, spinach, and onion.

professionals as well as other highly trained professionals. Another 25 percent of these immigrants reported their employment background as "executive, administrative, managerial, sales, or administrative support." Therefore, of all the Filipino immigrants who indicated their occupational skills to the INS in 2001, 73 percent reported a white-collar profession.

Nonetheless, many immigrants still find themselves working

in positions that might be considered of a lower caliber than what they had in the Philippines. Due to restrictive licensing laws that exist in many states, some professionals, such as dentists, may be first required to take additional schooling and testing before they can practice in their profession. Others find themselves in the position of starting over despite their years of experience in the Philippines. Immigrating attorneys, for example, may find their Philippine law training and background difficult to transfer to the United States due to the differences between the two legal systems.

In the Philippines, self-employment is quite common. Small

California, New York, and New Jersey are the top states for new Filipino Americans.

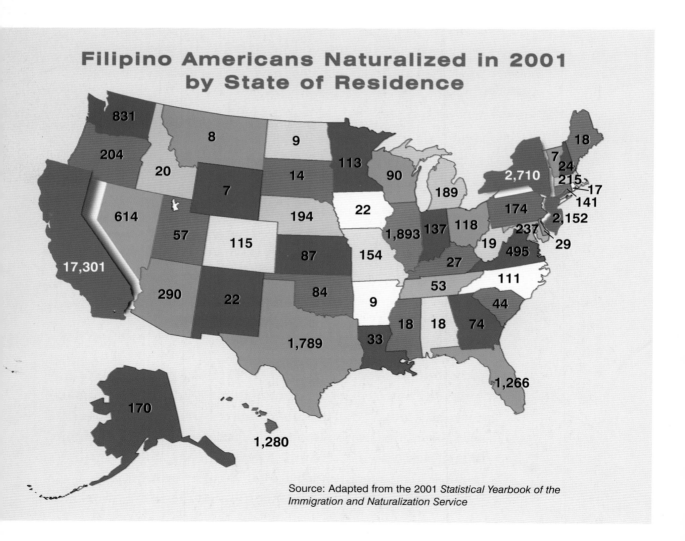

Filipino Americans Naturalized in 2001 by State of Residence

831
8
9
18
204
20
7
24
113
2,710
215
14
90
17
7
189
174
141
194
22
2,152
614
1,893 137 118
237
57
115
19
495
29
87
154
27
111
17,301
53
290
22
84
44
9
1,789
18 18 74
33
1,266
170
1,280

Source: Adapted from the 2001 *Statistical Yearbook of the Immigration and Naturalization Service*

Hawaii remains one of the most popular U.S. states in which Filipinos settle. Its popularity dates back to the early 20th century, when many Filipino laborers traveled to Hawaii to work on its sugar plantations.

enterprises abound in the forms of shops, stores, restaurants, and service providers. Filipinas, in particular, have a reputation as shrewd business managers and head many Philippine corporations. Even the stay-at-home mother of a large family may often run a part-time business in order to supplement her husband's income. However, fewer Filipino Americans are self-employed than their native countrymen, and Filipino Americans lag far behind other Asian Pacific groups such as Chinese Americans and Korean Americans in terms of self-employment. The inconsistency between Filipino business practices in the United States and those in the Philippines may puzzle some, but jobs are also much more plentiful in the United States. Thus, a Filipino American mother needing money, for example, may find it easier to gain employment with an existing company than start a business from scratch.

Household income for Filipino Americans is consistent with that of other Asian Pacific American households. Family members still depend on each other even after settling in North America, and it is not uncommon for grandparents, aunts, uncles, and adult children to reside in the home and contribute toward expenses.

Geographic Location

As might be expected, California is home to more Filipino Americans than any other state. Many immigrants and their families have simply chosen to remain in the state that is the traditional entry point for Filipinos coming to the U.S. mainland. Hawaii also continues to enjoy a strong Filipino presence, as it has since the early days of the sugar plantations.

In recent decades, other states have drawn significant numbers of Filipino immigrants as well. According to INS figures

At a Filipino-American Friendship Day celebration in Manila, a Filipina waves the flags of the United States and the Philippines. Friendship Day and similar celebrations are widely observed in both countries, and are especially popular among the many Filipino American social organizations in the U.S.

reported in 2001, all 50 states received at least a few of the Filipinos who came to the United States in the year 2001, but after California and Hawaii the most popular destinations were Illinois, New Jersey, Texas, and New York. These six states became home to two-thirds of all Filipino immigrants for that year. The top-five metropolitan areas among newcomers were Los Angeles, Chicago, Honolulu, San Diego, and Oakland.

Canada took in more than a quarter of a million immigrants from around the world in 2001; nearly half settled in and around the Toronto area. Filipinos followed this trend: out of approximately 13,000 Filipino immigrants, just over 6,000 went to Toronto. Another 3,000 went to Vancouver, reflecting the Filipino tendency to stay on the West Coast. The remaining 4,000 immigrants spread out among the nation's other cities and, to a lesser extent, its rural areas.

Both Canadian and American statistics show that Filipinos, like other immigrant groups, gravitate toward large cities. This is most likely due to an array of socio-economic factors. Housing and employment opportunities are often more readily available in metropolitan areas, and the diversity of ethnic groups results in them being more readily accepted and assimilated. Natives of Manila may simply feel more at home in a city environment. Of course, the choices of immigrants who preceded them undoubtedly play a role as well. Sponsored relatives of a Filipino doctor working in a city hospital will likely live very near (if not with) the doctor and his family.

Family Life and Social Activities

Filipinos have shown a remarkable adaptability to different cultures and lifestyles but, almost without exception, they retain the Filipino-style devotion to family. In the Philippines, personal goals and desires often take a back seat to family needs. Older children are expected to help their parents raise younger siblings. Extended family members also feel obligated to help and play an important role in everyday family life.

Upon becoming an adult, a son or daughter is more than

Keeping Filipino Americans Connected

Several print magazines and newsletters are specifically tailored to Filipino American readership. Perhaps the most successful of these is *Filipinas* magazine, a high-quality publication that mixes profiles of celebrities with coverage of important social issues such as racism and domestic abuse. *Filipinas* boasts that it is "the only nationally circulated, four-color, glossy, Filipino American magazine."

Publisher and editor Mona Lisa Yuchengco created *Filipinas* in 1992, while she was still a student. In the May 2002 issue, Yuchengco celebrated the magazine's 10th anniversary by reflecting back on the difficulties she faced over the years:

> Operating a business in the United States is so different from the Philippines, and more costly as well. I had to rely on all my skills and talents to make things work, and at the same time I had to bring out the best from the employees. I had to make them believe in the *Filipinas* dream as well so they would walk the extra mile with me. I wasn't always successful at this.

Yuchengco also urged her readers to play an active part in defining the future of Filipinos in America:

> We do not know what lies ahead for the Filipino American community. Our destiny in America will depend on us, on how we see and shape ourselves to become an integral, though unique, part of this society. We have seen our numbers grow (though not as much as we would like to) and with it comes a new responsibility for our role in American society.

welcome to remain living at home; in fact, it is encouraged. Filipino parents often express sadness over an adult child deciding to move out and become independent. Elder family members are granted the utmost respect. In some cases, familial dedication may be slightly less valued in America, but for the most part it remains essential.

Outmarriage, or marriage outside of one's own ethnic group, has long been a sign of assimilation in America. An examination of outmarriage rates in Los Angeles County in 1989 found that 47 percent of female immigrants from the Philippines had married non-Filipinos in the United States, with the rates increasing to 66 percent and 86 percent, respectively, for second- and third-generation Filipino American women.

Filipino immigrants react in different ways to the introduction of Western influences into family life. The majority of parents will at least tolerate changes in a child's attitudes, dress, and behavior, recognizing that a native-born American will most likely be torn between two cultures. Parents may not agree with the child's taste in music or sudden display of independence, but they generally will permit such explorations of identity provided that they are not destructive. At the same time, most parents will insist that their children acknowledge and honor their Filipino heritage and remain dedicated to their studies.

Filipino Americans are well known for forming and joining social organizations. These clubs, societies, and associations help satisfy the age-old Filipino need for social interaction. Groups are typically established on the basis of locale, occupation, or a common loyalty or experience. Popular Filipino American organizations include the United Filipino Council of Hawaii, the Association of Philippine Physicians in America, the Knights of Rizal, and the University of the Philippines Alumni Association of America, just to name a few.

Aside from offering social advantages, clubs and associations unite Filipino Americans and give them a stronger voice within the community and the nation. In recent years, some groups have recognized that they can wield even greater influence by banding together. This has led to the formation of umbrella organizations that may include all of the Filipino American groups in a given city or region. However, it has been difficult for Filipino Americans to organize politically. Interest in politics rarely extends beyond local issues directly affecting one's family or social organization.

Keeping in Touch

Filipino Americans often welcome chance encounters with their countrymen, or *kababayans*. Sharing fond memories of the islands can ease pangs of homesickness. Modern technology offers additional remedies: short-wave radio, satellite television, and the World Wide Web make the vast expanses of the Pacific seem to disappear.

Many Filipino Americans, particularly first-generation Filipino Americans, maintain close ties with their homeland. For some, it may merely involve reading the latest news via the Internet or a Philippine newspaper. For others, it is through frequent correspondence with friends and relatives. Many immigrants with family still in the Philippines routinely set aside a portion of their earnings to send "back home."

The practice of remitting funds to family members still in the archipelago is not unique to Filipino Americans; Filipinos living and working in other parts of the world send remittances as well. In fact, the Philippine economy has come to rely on this continual infusion of foreign cash from its sons and daughters working abroad. In 1996, it was estimated that one and a half million Filipinos living around the world forwarded 4.3 billion U.S. dollars to the islands during that year.

In 2001, President Gloria Macapagal-Arroyo officially thanked Filipino Americans for "boosting the Philippine economy and for shoring up our national stability through their foreign exchange remittances to Manila." She added:

> I shall ask them to continue their generosity. I shall ask them to visit the Philippines more often. And as they renew their acquaintance with their homeland, it would not be a bad idea to bring American friends along, or to urge Americans to taste our hospitality.

While most Filipinos living abroad send money back home, they may have different motivations for doing so. Filipinos working in the Middle East, for example, usually have no intention of settling there permanently and so do not send money back home for their family members' airfare to the Middle East. They are merely working overseas in order to make life better for their family. Once that goal has been accomplished, they will return home and perhaps use some of their foreign earnings to start a business or buy a house.

Filipinos who come to North America, on the other hand, usually intend to stay. While they certainly wish to improve the quality of life for family members left behind, they may also hope to someday have those family members join them in their new homeland.

5 OLD TRADITIONS, NEW CULTURE

Imagine yourself suddenly submerged in a fundamentally different society from your own. You might understand the language that is being spoken, and perhaps even identify with some of the activities you see. But the fact remains that you are a stranger and an outsider. The customs, values, and practices of the people surrounding you are dissimilar from your own. Now imagine that you must spend the rest of your life in this foreign world. Throughout history, Filipino and other immigrants seeking a better life have faced this challenge. Success depends primarily on the character of individuals and the hospitality offered by their new society.

Filipinos who arrived in North America prior to World War II certainly faced great a challenge. Most of them had come alone to work and send money back home to their families. Their only form of communication with loved ones in the Philippines was correspondence. Undoubtedly, these written words from family and friends must have stirred both fond memories of happier times and a great longing for home. There were few *kababayans* in their new homeland with whom to reminisce, and Filipino American restaurants and magazines were still decades away. Early arrivals likely had little choice but to relegate their former lifestyle to memory.

Today's Filipino immigrants have the opportunity to embrace their future without relinquishing all of their past. In addition to technological advances that facilitate routine communication

◄A Filipino in costume performs a dance with fire during a festival. Throughout the year, Filipino American communities hold festivals celebrating their cultural heritage and history, as well as religious holidays and special events involving family members.

Cockfighting, a popular sporting event in the Philippines, is one tradition that has not been preserved by Filipino immigrants in North America, where it is banned in Canada and 47 U.S. states.

and interaction with other Filipinos, the presence of sizable Filipino American communities means that traditional customs and rituals may continue to be observed.

Celebration and Fashion

Just as in the Philippines, parties and festivals are an important part of life for Filipino Americans. Philippine Independence Day (June 12) celebrates freedom from Spanish rule. Filipino-American Friendship Day (July 4) recognizes the day on which the United States granted the islands sovereignty. Rizal Day (December 30) honors the life of that national hero and martyr. Each of these holidays typically involves a formal celebration in Filipino American neighborhoods and communities.

Religious holidays also are a time to rejoice. Christmas, in particular, is a major event for Filipino Americans, who are predominantly Catholic. The Christmas celebration begins long before Christmas Day with a series of religious services, banquets, and gift exchanges. Easter is also a time of great festivity and pageantry.

Traditional Filipino wedding rites can involve tying a cord around the bride and groom to symbolize their union. Some

Filipino American couples incorporate this ritual into their church ceremony as a tribute to their homeland. In the Philippines, the groom's parents are expected to pay the reception expenses, but this custom does not appear to be widely followed by Filipinos living in North America. Providing food for guests to take home after the reception, however, is a tradition that Filipino Americans continue to practice.

Birthdays, anniversaries, and the arrival or departure of a friend or family member are additional reasons to celebrate. The Filipino tradition of arriving late to a party is not intended to insult the hosts. Filipinos are extremely conscious of appearances, and by being late the guests may avoid having the appearance of being overly anxious.

A typical Philippine village spends a considerable amount of time preparing for its annual festival, which is a celebration of life and togetherness. Family members from around the archipelago return to their native village and participate in the fiesta. The month of May is a popular time for festivals since it comes just before the rainy season begins. An abundance of food, colorful decoration, and spirited games are trademarks of the village fiesta. In one traditional game, contestants attempt to scale a greased bamboo pole and reach a prize, usually money, at the top. Competitions in singing, oration, and cockfighting may also be held.

Filipino American festivals may not have events such as pole climbing and cockfighting, but they are just as lively as the fiestas back home. Parties often coincide with holidays such as Filipino-American Friendship Day in July and Rizal Day in December. Popular American dishes complement traditional ethnic cooking, as picnickers compete in volleyball, basketball, and soccer tournaments. Fiestas may be sponsored by a single Filipino American organization, or by a group of organizations. In addition to bringing people together, these festivals provide fundraising opportunities for the sponsoring organizations, allowing them to host other events throughout the year.

In Olympia, Washington, the Filipino American Community

of South Puget Sound holds an annual celebration of Filipino heritage. Activities are centered around the longstanding Filipino tradition of honoring the elderly, group president Rufino Ignacio told *The Olympian* newspaper. "This is our modest way of expressing respect and admiration for our seniors, for their love and wisdom," he said. He added that festival organizers also try to educate the young about their heritage: "This is our way to instill the beautiful heritage of the Philippines into the American young people, our children."

As the number of Filipino Americans has grown, some festivals have taken on national and even international significance. In August 2002, Filipinos from around the world gathered in San Francisco for the first Global Filipino Community Networking Convention. Touted as "the largest gathering to date of Filipinos from around the globe," the two-day event featured a long list of notable guest speakers, a basketball tournament, and a community parade. Such national conventions are beneficial to all Filipino Americans because they attract public attention, and aid in dispelling notions of the "invisibility" of the group.

Filipino Americans tend to dress like most other Americans, but they also maintain a few articles of clothing from their native land. For men, the quintessential Filipino fashion statement is the *barong*—a white shirt with a band collar and long tails. *Barongs* can be found throughout the Philippines and Filipino American communities in varying quality and cost. A long-sleeved

Traditional Filipina fashion is known for its elaborate jewelry and colorful embroidered dresses. Many Filipino American women import silk and satins from the homeland to make their own dresses.

barong is considered formal attire; it is always worn over the pants and never tucked in. Filipino American women have more options with formal wear. Their dresses are usually very colorful and ornately embroidered, and are often handmade from silks and satins imported from the Philippines.

Arts and Entertainment

Since the earliest days of immigration to North America, Filipinos have eloquently expressed themselves in writing. With passionate prose, they have described their experiences as "hyphenated Americans." The first such author was Carlos Bulosan (1911–56), who immigrated to America during the Great Depression.

Unable to find work, Bulosan endured prejudice and harsh living conditions, eventually contracting tuberculosis. During his two-year hospitalization, he educated himself and began writing. In 1946, he published his most famous book, *America Is in the Heart*, a semi-autobiographical story about the struggles of Filipino migrant workers on the West Coast. Bulosan is considered the quintessential Filipino American writer, and his writings are still carefully analyzed today in courses in Asian American studies. *America Is in the Heart* has been widely read by both Filipinos and non-Filipinos for its insights on the experiences of the Filipinos referred to as the Pinoy generation.

The San Francisco Public Library acknowledged the contributions of Filipino authors by launching its Filipino American Center in April 1996. The center houses numerous volumes of both classic and contemporary Filipino novels, plays, poems, short stories, and nonfiction. Videos, music, children's material, and reference resources are also available in English and Tagalog. Since public library services are generally unavailable in the Philippines, some American libraries have implemented outreach programs. These programs target newly arrived Filipino immigrants, introducing them to the many beneficial services American libraries have to offer.

In addition to making forays into the world of literature,

Filipino Americans also showcase their talents on the stage. Some metropolitan areas host a Filipino American performing arts center for plays, concerts, poetry readings, and other presentations. For example, the Filipino American community in San Francisco's Bay Area supports the Bindlestiff Studio, a small theater with a full schedule of events, including a semiannual Filipino rock festival. When city plans for the Bindlestiff building jeopardized the tiny studio's future, Filipino Americans in the area rallied together and saved the studio from closing down.

Hollywood traditionally has offered few opportunities to Filipino actors and directors. Both have found themselves relegated to minor films with exposure limited to the Asian American markets. But recent successes by Asian filmmakers may help Filipinos make some breakthroughs. The achievements of Taiwanese director Ang Lee set an example that Filipino directors have hoped to emulate. His movie *Crouching Tiger, Hidden Dragon* garnered four Oscars in 2001 and received ten nominations—a record for a foreign film.

Filipino American director David Maquiling had to overcome major hurdles before making the types of films that interested him. In a 2001 interview for National Public Radio, Maquiling described the resistance he faced:

> There was just a rejection of me as a Filipino American making a film that had a Caucasian cast. And on the one hand, absolutely I understand and completely agree with the idea that we do need a greater physical representation on screen. At the same time, I do have a problem with people who think that as an Asian American I can only deal very specifically with Asian-American themes.

Dancing, Displays, and Pageantry

Ethnic dance demonstrations are among the more popular methods for young Filipino Americans to explore their heritage. For nearly half a century, Filipino American troupes across the country have performed traditional dances for audiences of all ages and ethnic backgrounds. The most renowned

Members of the Kalanguya tribe participate in an annual festival in Sante Fe, the Philippines. Filipino Americans remember their heritage through similar celebrations, and many dedicate themselves to learning the ethnic dances and martial arts of the homeland.

of these groups, the Filipino Youth Activities Drill Team of Seattle, has been delighting crowds with precision demonstrations since 1957. Demand for performances steadily increased in the mid-1990s, resulting in an explosion in the number of Filipino dance clubs and organizations.

A standard at these performances is the ancient *tinikling* dance. Two long bamboo poles are laid parallel and a person kneels at each end. As the two people at the end repeatedly slap the poles together, barefoot performers nimbly dance and jump in between, their toes narrowly avoiding the clashing timber beneath. The symbolism behind this dance is open to debate. Some say the dancer mimics a bird hopping through the fields of the Philippines, searching for food as it carefully avoids the farmer's traps. Others offer a culturally themed metaphor, arguing that the dance has come to represent the deftness of Filipinos as they hop between the clashing Eastern and Western worlds.

Filipino music largely reflects the influence of Spanish colonization, but some examples of indigenous music still remain. In Mindanao, gongs, drums, and bamboo flutes are used to produce lively melodies with a distinctly Asian sound. Just as with Filipino dance, interest in native Filipino music has risen over the past decade in both the United States and Canada.

Filipino martial arts have also received much attention in recent years. For centuries, villagers learned martial arts to defend themselves from rival clans and invaders. Since these techniques had to be learned quickly, and by people of varying skill, a resulting characteristic of Filipino martial arts is simplicity. Present-day students are encouraged to focus on only those moves with which they feel most comfortable. Filipino martial arts are commonly associated with "stick fighting," but this is a misnomer, as many of the techniques are just as effective with empty hands. During Spanish occupation, martial arts were outlawed but training was secretly passed down through the generations. Today, many Filipino Americans take martial arts training for the threefold benefit of exercise, self-defense, and understanding their heritage.

Filipinos place an importance on physical attractiveness. Many Filipinos equate beauty with success, prosperity,

At a coronation ceremony held in Quezon City, Philippines, Kim So-Yun of South Korea is crowned Miss Asia Pacific 2002. Beauty pageants are popular among many Filipino immigrants, who follow the pageants held in the homeland as well as those sponsored by local organizations.

The Alvarado Project

Ricardo Alvarado emigrated from the Philippines in 1928. He lived alone and worked at menial jobs until the outbreak of World War II, at which time he enlisted in the First Filipino Regiment of the U.S. Army as a medical technician. After the war, Alvarado remained in the army, serving for 20 years at the Presidio, a military outpost in San Francisco. On a trip to the Philippines in 1959, he met the woman who soon became his wife. They raised a family, living happily in San Francisco until Alvarado died of leukemia in 1976.

Later, while going through his things, Alvarado's daughter Janet made a startling discovery. Her father had developed a passion for photography while living alone in America during the 1940s and 1950s, and he snapped thousands of pictures of Filipino American life. Alvarado's collection vividly portrays the Filipino American experience on the West Coast during that era. Images of field laborers and shopkeepers, and beauty pageants and cockfights, offer a rare glimpse into a largely undocumented period. Janet arranged the photographs into a collection and began displaying them at Filipino American events across the country. She also formed the Alvarado Project to preserve and promote her father's work.

In November 2002, the Alvarado collection went on display at the Smithsonian National Museum of American History in Washington, D.C. Entitled "Through My Father's Eyes," this one-of-a-kind exhibition was described by the Smithsonian as "a rich trove of historically significant and visually arresting images." After its stay in the Smithsonian, Alvarado's exhibition will travel to museums nationwide and continue to raise public awareness of the Filipino American experience.

The Alvarado Project website (www.thealvaradoproject.com) lets visitors know where they can see exhibits of Ricardo Alvardo's photograph collection, which documents Filipino American life during the 1940s and 1950s.

and happiness. From a very young age, Filipinas learn to always look their best. Pageants are held throughout the archipelago, and winning Filipinas are afforded celebrity status.

Beauty pageants are also prevalent in Filipino American communities, usually under the sponsorship of a social club. But in addition to appearance and charm, the contestants' fundraising abilities are usually a factor in selecting a queen. The judge's choice of a pageant winner is often cause for spirited debate, and occasionally, downright animosity.

Keeping Shop

In his book *Locating Filipino Americans: Ethnicity and the Cultural Politics of Space* (2000), author Rick Bonus stresses an important role played by Asian grocery stores in maintaining Filipino identity. Bonus interviewed dozens of Filipino shoppers at Asian food stores in Los Angeles and San Diego to determine why they patronized those establishments. He found that in addition to the nostalgia elicited by Filipino items, shoppers also felt a sense of community through the family-owned stores.

"It's enjoyable to shop here because we can mix it with conversation," one woman told Bonus. "I see those I know. And then we tell each other stories." Another patron said, "It's like what used to be the kind of stores in the Philippines. There's a

Learning New Shopping Habits

Filipino Americans are part of the burgeoning Asian American consumer segment of the population. Since the early 1990s, corporations have worked tirelessly to capture a piece of this $250-billion market. The earliest of these efforts made the mistake of using the same advertisements and promotions for all Asian groups. Marketers soon realized that an advertisement that persuades Korean or Chinese shoppers might be ineffective or even insulting to Filipino buyers. Today, promotional material is tailored to each ethnic group and is often presented in that group's native tongue. Marketing firm studies show that 66 percent of Filipino immigrants prefer advertisements in Filipino to those in English.

mix of gossip in the stores. Often, it's like that here." Buyers also pointed to the availability of products that cannot be found on the shelves of American supermarkets. Without these items, many traditional meals that Filipino American families enjoy could not be prepared.

In addition to purchasing foodstuffs, shoppers obtain valuable information posted on bulletin boards about job openings at Filipino businesses, property for sale, and upcoming social events. The market can also serve as a meeting place for men and women wishing to date within their own ethnic group. Stores become cultural linchpins in those areas where Filipino Americans are widely dispersed, with some customers routinely traveling 20 miles (32 kilometers) or more to get their favorite products and the latest community news.

Working Together

In Tagalog it is called *bayanihan*, the art of working together to achieve a common goal. When a Filipino farmer needs help harvesting his crops, friends and neighbors from the village may lend a hand. Likewise, the farmer may offer his assistance when other villagers are in need. Philippine history, rife with natural disaster and foreign aggression, fostered this system of cooperation and mutual support that continues to thrive today.

Many Filipino immigrants wrestle with the issue of cultural identity. The innocent but direct inquiry "What nationality are you?" gives them pause. Should their reply be "Filipino," "Filipino American," or simply "American"? It is a personal choice, and one that is usually only arrived at after much introspection. Recent immigrants may still consider themselves Filipinos, but they are also eager to embrace aspects of their new culture. Conversely, most Filipino Americans who have been naturalized as U.S. citizens still wish to maintain a connection with the Philippines, even if it is only in their thoughts.

6 PROBLEMS AND CHALLENGES

Though most Filipino Americans consider themselves fortunate and far better off than they were in the Philippines, their new lives are not without difficulty. Filipinos migrating to North America are presented with a series of challenges they may not have expected, including culture shock, prejudice, and financial struggles.

Culture Shock

The term "culture shock" refers to the stress one feels upon being immersed in a new and different social environment. Strange practices, ideals, and customs may overwhelm newcomers and leave them longing for home. Undoubtedly, all Filipinos experience some degree of culture shock upon their arrival in North America. Most people who travel to a foreign country, even if just for a vacation, feel somewhat out of place. How much culture shock do Filipino immigrants experience, and how long does it last?

Of course, because Filipinos have a distinct advantage over many other immigrant groups in terms of language, they may experience less culture shock. While they may not be familiar with all current slang and idioms, most Filipinos have a solid grasp of English and can communicate effectively. Conversely, immigrants from non-English speaking countries naturally find the language a significant barrier and a major source of culture shock.

◀ A protester on the University of California campus in Berkeley collects signatures for a petition demanding the removal of Proposition 209, a 1996 initiative that banned affirmative action at universities and other state institutions.

The long-established Filipino passion for American culture provides another advantage. Familiarity with the latest Hollywood movie stars and the rules of sports like basketball and baseball can enhance a Filipino's sense of belonging. Likewise, since the Philippine government and educational system are based on American models, those institutions are somewhat less mysterious for Filipinos than for other immigrants.

Certain aspects of American culture may alarm new arrivals, however. The frank demeanor of many Americans may shock some Filipinos. One approach to settling into immigrant life is to find a balance between traditional homeland values such as *hiya* (shame) and *amor-propio* (self-esteem), and the direct approach that is customary to Americans and Canadians.

Prejudice

On August 10, 1999, a Filipino immigrant and part-time postal employee was gunned down while delivering the mail in the vicinity of a Los Angeles Jewish Community Center targeted by white supremacist Buford O. Furrow, Jr. The 39-year-old immigrant, Joseph Santos Ileto, had come to America in 1974. He was known as a pleasant man who worked two jobs to support his family. According to a CNN report, Furrow stated that he would not have shot Ileto if the mail carrier had been white.

Fortunately, Filipino Americans are rarely victims of this type of hate crime, though there have been reported cases of discrimination. In 2002, Filipino Americans were among a group of 2,000 Asian Americans in Washington State pursuing a class-action lawsuit against Boeing, one of the world's largest aircraft manufacturers. The suit alleged that Asian American employees at Boeing were paid less and received fewer promotions than their white coworkers, and that the aviation giant took advantage of the Asians' reluctance to complain in its employment decisions.

There have been other protests made by Filipinos who believe they have been unfairly treated at the workplace. When the

September 2001 terrorist attacks prompted the government to federalize all airport security screening positions, Filipinos working at San Francisco International Airport had to scramble to keep their jobs. In November 2001, Congress passed the Aviation and Transportation Security Act, which prohibited non-U.S. citizens from being airport security workers. According to an online edition of *AsianWeek*, the legislation affected the 800 non-U.S. citizens who were employed by the San Francisco airport. A large portion of this group was Filipino.

Some of these Filipino workers took action by filing a lawsuit against the Department of Transportation, claiming that the new federal hiring practices were discriminatory. Under a new program announced in late 2002, Filipinos who had been non-U.S. citizens before could now be rehired, provided they met the federal guidelines for security screeners. However, many individuals could not meet requirements by the announced deadline.

A U.S. postal employee carries a rose in memory of coworker Joseph Santos Ileto, an Filipino immigrant who was gunned down in August 1999. Ileto's murderer, a white supremacist, stated he would not have shot the man if he had been white. The tragedy was a rare instance of race hatred against Filipinos in the United States.

A former employee of San Francisco International Airport wipes her tears at a rally for airport security workers in February 2002, four months after the Aviation and Transportation Security Act was passed. The act, which came in the wake of the September 2001 terrorist attacks in New York and Washington, D.C., prohibited non-U.S. citizens from being airport security workers and subsequently terminated the employment of a number of Filipinos.

The Filipino Immigrant Family

The range and quality of employment opportunities have shifted significantly throughout the years of Filipino immigration. Prior to World War II, Filipino Americans mostly worked at manual labor. While these jobs were abundant, they paid low wages. In the decades following the war, well-paying and fulfilling professional jobs, such as those in the health care industry, became available. These opportunities attracted, and continue to attract, a large number of Filipino doctors and nurses.

However, in recent years it appears that a small divide has

grown between the success rates of Filipino immigrants and second-generation Filipino Americans, or children of Filipino immigrants. Immigrants born in the Philippines fare better in school than American-born Filipinos, according to a review of 1990 U.S. Census data by Barbara Posadas. Researchers labor to find a conclusive reason for this difference, but a popular theory focuses on the overriding importance placed on education in the Philippines versus the more relaxed attitudes demonstrated in America. When both parents (and in some cases, older siblings) are employed full-time, children often do not receive the attention and supervision they would have received in the Philippines.

In addition, some Filipino American children who lack parental supervision fall into trouble within peer groups known as *barcadas*. In the Philippines, *barcadas* are groups in which young people gather to socialize. These groups teach important socialization skills and also serve as an introduction to the opposite sex, as male and female *barcadas* will go out on group dates before eventually pairing off into couples.

In the United States, while a number of the *barcadas* have remained harmless, other have evolved into gangs that stray into the realm of violent crime. Police departments in several major cities have reported the existence of rival Filipino gangs.

Second-generation Filipino Americans are slightly worse off financially than Filipino immigrants, and are also less likely to hold professional and managerial professions. Another reason for this discrepancy is that many children of those Filipino doctors and nurses who found employment during the 1960s and 1970s have not followed their parents into the healthcare field.

Elderly Filipino immigrants frequently come to America because their families have chosen to do so. Adapting to a new culture is more difficult for them than for their children and grandchildren. Sandwiched between young and old are the middle-aged wage earners of the family. In addition to their own difficulties, they must take on the problems of both their children and their parents.

Undocumented Immigrants

The overwhelming majority of Filipinos living in the United States and Canada are either naturalized citizens or eligible noncitizens. Undocumented immigrants from the Philippines are most often students, workers, or tourists who have overstayed their visas. The terrorist attacks of September 11, 2001, gave higher priority to deportations of individuals who did not have legal status, particularly from the Middle and Far East. Ties between the al-Qaeda terror network and Philippine rebel groups have made some undocumented Filipino immigrants targets of greater attention for federal authorities.

William Manalastas and his family were among the first Filipino Americans targeted for deportation during the subsequent crackdown. Manalastas, his wife, and their four young daughters had entered the United States in the early 1990s under tourist visas, and remained in New Jersey long after the visas had expired. Ordered to leave by an immigration judge in 1995, the Manalastas family instead moved to Elizabethtown, Kentucky, where they had hoped to live quietly, undetected by immigration officials. Manalastas and his wife obtained employment and the girls enrolled in school. They joined a Catholic church in their community. It appeared that the Manalastases had escaped deportation.

The family's situation changed suddenly after the terrorist attacks. In March 2002, William Manalastas was arrested and detained as part of an INS sweep. He was returned to the Philippines in June 2002, though his wife and daughters were permitted to remain in the United States while their status was considered. Manalastas and his wife acknowledged their mistakes, saying they recognized the need for immigration laws and enhanced security. They only hoped to be a family once again and remain in the small Kentucky town they now considered home.

A common problem for Filipino Americans who are legal immigrants is the lengthy process of bringing family members from the Philippines to the United States. Each year, the number of Filipinos seeking to enter the U.S. consistently exceeds the

Two alleged members of the Filipino Muslim extremist group Abu Sayyaf, which some believe has connections with the al-Qaeda international terrorist network, sit in a holding pen in September 2000. The apprehensions of the men were part of a Philippine clampdown on Abu Sayyaf.

number of immigrant visas available, resulting in a severe backlog. Relatives of Filipino Americans have, in some cases, waited nearly two decades to join their loved ones. The extended wait may have helped spur some Filipinos' relatives to immigrate to Canada. Though families are still separated, at least visits across the U.S.-Canadian border are much easier than traveling across the Pacific Ocean. However, it may not be possible for the individual to immigrate under Canada's system.

7 THE FUTURE

Filipino Americans have good reason for optimism. Though some difficulties remain, many major obstacles have been eliminated and life today is far better than it was for previous generations. Of course, as old problems are resolved, new ones invariably emerge. Maintaining opportunities for immigrants and children will be among the goals of Filipino Americans in the coming decades.

Growth of Filipino Immigration

Latin America continues to be the largest contributor of immigrants to the United States, and there is little evidence that the pattern will change. Mexico, in particular, leads as a supplier of immigrants. In 2000, the U.S. Census Bureau determined that more than a quarter of the foreign-born population originated from Mexico. China was a distant second, and closely following it was the Philippines.

In March 2000, the U.S. foreign-born population stood at 28.4 million (approximately 10 percent of the entire U.S. population). Filipino immigrants accounted for roughly 1.2 million, or 4.2 percent, of the immigrant population. But in 1970, when there were 9.6 million immigrants living in the United States, only 185,000 (or 1.9 percent) were Filipinos. These figures demonstrate two distinct trends: there has been an increase in immigration to the United States during recent decades, and Filipinos played an important part in that increase.

◀ Census results indicate that succeeding generations of Filipino Americans and Filipino Canadians are likely to be greater in number than the present-day population. As of 2000, there were 1.2 million Filipino Americans born in the United States. In Canada, recent legislation has allowed for the entry of Filipinos in greater numbers.

Undoubtedly, the Filipino American population will continue to grow at a steady pace. Only dramatic changes to U.S. immigration policy could seriously jeopardize further growth, and then only if those changes obstructed the longstanding objective of reuniting families. This appears unlikely in the near future. The "war on terrorism" has placed a renewed emphasis on preventing illegal entry, and future immigration laws will more likely address that issue than the legal immigration processes that allow families to reunite.

Filipino Americans who were born in the United States number 1.2 million, according to the 2000 U.S. Census Bureau, and their role in Filipino immigration cannot be overlooked. As the children of immigrants, most maintain a strong association with their Filipino heritage. And, as one-half of the Filipino American population, they could outnumber immigrants in the coming years, representing a landmark for the history of Filipino migration to the United States.

The future of Filipino immigration may be even brighter in Canada, where the enactment of the Immigration and Refugee Protection Act in 2002 reconfirmed the country's commitment to newcomers. In 2001, there were 239,160 Filipino immigrants residing in Canada, or 4.2 percent of the immigrant population, according to that year's census. Between the years 1996 and 2001, Filipinos accounted for 5.8 percent of the new arrivals to Canada, raising the overall Filipino immigrant population to over 239,000. The numbers of Filipinos will likely continue to expand as the Immigration and Refugee Protection Act is expected to improve the prospects for those wishing to move to the country.

Filipinos in the U.S. Military

Filipino Americans historically have not gone out of their way to make themselves highly visible in the American public arena. Throughout their history in the United States, they have tended to focus more on matters of the family and community than social or political movements. Since the early 1990s,

Filipino American clubs and organizations have banded together and worked toward common goals. Though far from realizing a unified voice, Filipino Americans have begun to exert more political influence.

The Filipino tradition of military service continues, with

Immigrants and the Economy

The arrival of foreign workers often raises concerns of diminishing job opportunities for native-born workers. Indeed, some may think that more workers results in fewer job openings. However, studies focusing on the U.S. labor market and immigration patterns are beginning to prove otherwise. Analysts are paying particularly close attention to the 1990s—a decade marked by both robust economic expansion and soaring immigration figures.

Utilizing Census 2000 statistical data, researchers at Northeastern University discovered that immigrants play a key role in creating and sustaining economic growth. The 2002 study found that foreign workers help avert critical labor shortages in booming industries, thus prolonging periods of economic development. Newcomers also foster innovation by bringing different skills and added diversity to the workplace. Rather than steal employment away from natural citizens, immigrants instead participate in an economic process that creates more jobs for all. Immigrants create jobs by spending money for services and products produced by others, and by starting businesses, saving, and investing in the economy.

It is likely the Northeastern Unversity study's results did not surprise managers in the health care industry, who have been relying on Filipinos to fill nursing shortages for over half a century. Nor would health care managers be surprised by the study's finding that many immigrants possess advanced job skills. "New immigrants filled a relatively high share of jobs in professional, skilled blue-collar, and production/assembler positions, including many engineering, scientific, and skilled craft positions," said Paul Harrington, associate director of Northeastern's Center for Labor Market Studies.

As the enormous "baby boom" generation continues to leave the workforce for retirement, Filipino Americans and other immigrant groups are joining native-born employees to fill the void. This transition will clearly demonstrate the critical importance of immigrant workers. In the future, countries may need to actively recruit newcomers in order to stay competitive in the global marketplace.

Filipino Americans rising to the highest ranks of the U.S. armed forces. Commenting on Filipino American contributions to the Second Gulf War in Iraq, Rodel Rodis wrote in the *San Francisco Chronicle*: "Filipino American heroes from the war in Iraq are changing the image of Filipinos across America. From Joseph Menusa to OJ Santa Maria to Joseph Hudson, their stories embrace the full spectrum of what is considered to be the best American ideals of courage, sacrifice and death."

Many people do not realize that noncitizens can serve in the U.S. military, but in fact in 2003 there were over 30,000 who served. Filipinos comprised 20.6 percent of all noncitizens in the U.S. military, according to the U.S. Department of Defense. Marine Gunnery Sergeant Joseph Menusa, a Filipino immigrant, died in the Second Gulf War. He was granted U.S. citizenship following his death.

Marine Lance Corporal OJ Santa Maria, 21, severely injured in Iraq, underwent three surgeries in a Maryland hospital.

Devout Catholics in the Philippine province of Bulacan reenact the crucifixion of Jesus. A large percentage of Catholic Filipinos continue practicing their faith in North America churches, although many discover that the churches' rituals and ceremonies differ from those of Philippine churches.

According to the *San Francisco Chronicle*, on a special day in which he was sworn in as a U.S. citizen, he had tears in his eyes. President George W. Bush, visiting him in the hospital, told him: "We're proud to have you as an American."

Filipinos also protect the public as police officers, emergency workers, and judges. In the private sector, Filipino Americans run multimillion-dollar businesses and participate in the management of major corporations. Such advancements in the workplace have led to a greater appreciation of Filipino Americans and their countless contributions to society. As the Filipino American community continues to expand and gain prominence, interest in Filipino culture is likely to grow. Americans have already expressed a curiosity in native Filipino music, dancing, and martial arts. The growing number of Filipino Americans in the entertainment industry is another sign of their growing visibility, as is the increase in restaurants specializing in Filipino cuisine. While these developments are welcomed by Filipino Americans, in the future the most important aspects of their lives will continue to be devotion to their families and their children's future.

Most Filipino immigrants have a strong religious background and are eager to continue that spiritual life in their new country. For an overwhelming majority, this means joining a nearby Roman Catholic church. Filipino Americans are known to actively participate in church events: singing in the choir, organizing fundraisers, and volunteering as altar servers. They may also send their children to Catholic school despite the additional financial burden.

The Catholic Church in the Philippines still has much of the same character it had four centuries ago. It has a loyal following and has preserved many traditional rites, yet its administration lacks structure. New arrivals are often surprised by many of the established practices of North American Catholicism. Formal church membership, marriage preparation classes, and Sunday donation envelopes all represent a level of bureaucratic organization with which many Filipino Catholics are unaccustomed.

Also, many of the rites, ceremonies, and processions that Filipinos associate with their faith are absent in the churches they have adopted.

New Challenges

Filipino immigrants of the 21st century are confronted with many of the same problems as their predecessors, but they also face new challenges. Unsuspecting newcomers may fall victim to fraud. For example, they become easy prey for swindlers who promise to find ideal housing, secure quality employment, or handle immigration paperwork. Upon making a sizable down payment, the trusting immigrant often never sees this person again, or subsequently finds that the services rendered are far less than what had been promised. Since many Filipino immigrants already have family members and other viable connections residing in North America, they are less susceptible to scam artists than some other ethnic groups, but nonetheless they occasionally find themselves cheated.

Other illegal operations have far more serious ramifications for Filipino immigrants than financial loss. In June 2002, the U.S. Department of State released a report on the worldwide epidemic of "people trafficking." In what amounts to a modern form of slavery, traffickers lure poverty-stricken citizens of developing countries to more prosperous countries with promises of high-paying jobs and a better life. Upon entering the country, which is often through illegal means, these immigrants are forced to work in sweatshops, the sex trade, or as domestic servants.

The State Department included the Philippines as one of the countries responsible for some of the estimated 700,000 people that are trafficked each year around the world. The Philippines is classified as a "Tier 2" country, which means that its government has taken steps to address the trafficking problem but has had only marginal success. The majority of Filipinos ensnared by traffickers are sent to other Asian countries, but an unknown number eventually arrive in North America for exploitation. Chinese citizens are also trafficked to the Philippines. From there, they may be trafficked again to other Pacific Islands nations or to North America, according to the State Department report.

Another issue concerning Filipino immigrants is the blooming international matchmaking industry, also known as the "mail-order bride" industry. According to a report on international matchmaking organizations delivered in February 1999 to U.S. Congress by the INS, Asia is one of the two regions that are the largest suppliers of mail-order brides. The report also stated that "the Philippines provides a large number of the Asian listings, despite the fact that 'mail-order bride' activities have been illegal there since 1986." The expansion of the Internet has greatly facilitated this form of international matchmaking, which is legal in North America.

Some Filipino immigrants make the decision to move back to their island home. Many returning Filipinos believe that with the country's decline in government corruption and a recent period of economic growth, they may find a better life than the one they first left behind.

Going Back, Looking Forward

According to the 2000 INS *Statistical Yearbook*, roughly 19,000 immigrants returned to the Philippines during the 1980s, or 3.5 percent of the Filipinos who immigrated to the United States during that decade. While experts have not recorded the specific reasons why these Filipinos have returned, it is possible to imagine some of their motivations: a longing for family, great financial pressure, and a general sense of isolation.

Those returning to the Philippines may find a different country from the one they left behind for North America. Life in the rural regions may change slowly, but urban areas evolve rapidly. The Philippines appears to be entering another pivotal period. The scourge of government corruption appears to be declining. Technological advancements are gradually spreading outward from Manila. Current economic conditions hint at a period of resurgence. The United States and other countries are

President George W. Bush and President Gloria Macapagal-Arroyo of the Philippines meet in Washington, D.C., in May 2003. Although Arroyo is finding some success implementing economic and political reform in the Philippines, experts predict that in the years ahead the numbers of Filipinos searching for a brighter financial future in North America will remain high.

providing much-needed financial support to the Philippine government. The implementation of a sound economic plan, plus the effective use of international aid, could result in a period of sustained growth.

Rosy predictions about the Philippines' future must be accompanied by a healthy skepticism. The economy has shown signs of vitality in the past, only to slip into periods of lethargy. An ever-growing schism between the Muslim population in the South and the Christian majority could result in more violence and bloodshed, as well as scare off tourism and the revenue it brings.

If the administration of Gloria Macapagal-Arroyo and her successors manage to break the grip of poverty on their country, immigration to North America would be less popular of an option for Filipinos. However, complete economic reform is not yet in sight, and so Filipino Americans can expect to see their ranks grow in coming years. Future arrivals will build their new lives on a foundation laid down by previous generations of immigrants. This framework is based on social equity, acceptance, and increasing visibility, but there is always room for improvement.

What does it mean to be Filipino American? No single response can sufficiently answer that question. Filipino Americans will likely always hold onto certain traits. An unwavering devotion to family, a positive outlook on life, and a highly adaptive nature will likely define future Filipino immigrants to the United States and Canada just as they have done in the past. Such traits ensure that the Filipino American story will remain a positive chapter in immigration studies for generations to come.

Angela Perez Baraquio (1977–), a second-generation Filipina and elementary school teacher in Hawaii. She became the first Asian American to be crowned Miss America in 2001, and has championed youth education issues.

Benjamin Cayetano (1939–), the first Filipino American to serve as state governor. He served for 12 years in Hawaii's legislature and 8 years as lieutenant governor before he was elected governor in 1994; he was reelected in 1998.

Howard Chua-Eoan (1959–), Filipino American journalist and former senior editor at *People* magazine. He became the news director of *Time* magazine in 2002, and has received several journalism awards.

Roman Gabriel (1940–), the son of a Filipino immigrant and a former professional football star. He was quarterback for the Los Angeles Rams for 10 seasons, broke a number of team passing records, and was voted the NFL's Most Valuable Player in 1969.

Jessica Hagedorn (1949–), novelist, poet, and performance artist, arguably the best Filipino American author of the modern era. Her 1990 novel *Dogeaters* received accolades for its gritty portrait of urban life in the Philippines during the Marcos era, and *The Gangster of Love*, published in 1996, highlights the struggles of Filipino immigrants in San Francisco and New York.

Loida Nicolas Lewis (1942–), a Philippine-trained attorney who immigrated to New York in the late 1960s. She became the first foreign-educated Asian woman to pass the New York State bar exam and has authored several books for Filipinos on U.S. immigration law.

Dr. Eleanor Concepcion ("Connie") Mariano (1955–), U.S. Navy doctor and White House physician during the Clinton administration. In 2000, she became the first Asian American woman to attain the rank of rear admiral.

Dr. Rey D. Pagtakhan (1935–), children's lung specialist who immigrated to Canada in 1968. He won a seat in the House of Commons in 1988 and was reelected to a fourth term in 2000. In 2002, he was appointed minister for veterans affairs and secretary of state (science, research, and development).

FAMOUS FILIPINO AMERICANS/CANADIANS

Veronica Pedrosa (1972–), television news broadcaster who fled the Philippines with her family in the 1970s because her mother wrote an unauthorized biography of Imelda Marcos. She reported for the British Broadcasting Company (BBC) before she joined CNN and became anchor for *Asia Tonight*, a prime-time news program broadcast live across Asia.

Lou Diamond Phillips (1962–), Filipino American actor who became a Hollywood celebrity in 1987 after portraying 1950s rock musician Ritchie Valens in the hit film *La Bamba*. He has also directed for the film and stage and has received public accolades for his dedication to ending world hunger.

Lieutenant General Edward Soriano (1947–), Filipino American officer in the U.S. Army, has served in Korea, the Persian Gulf, and Bosnia. He has received numerous service and achievement medals, and in 2002 he became the first native-born Filipino to reach the rank of lieutenant general.

Velma Veloria (1950–), the first Asian American woman in the Washington State House of Representatives, she has introduced legislation supporting economic development, women's issues, and minority businesses.

GLOSSARY

amor-propio—in Filipino, a person's self-image, how he or she hopes to be seen by others.

Bahala na—an expression that means "leave it to God." It conveys the belief that problems beyond one's control will eventually work themselves out.

balikbayan—means "homecoming," refers to someone who returns to visit the Philippines. *Balikbayans* are expected to bring gifts for friends and family upon their return.

barong—a long, collared white shirt with long slits along the sides that is never tucked into the pants. It is worn by men for formal events.

bayanihan—the Tagalog term for working together to achieve a common goal.

hiya—a sense of shame. Filipinos who fails at a task or behave inappropriately bring *hiya* to themselves and their family.

jeepney—jeeps driven by Filipinos that were left behind by the U.S. Army after World War II.

kababayan—the Filipino word for "countryman."

Pinoy—"old timer"; a nickname for the earliest Filipino immigrants, who came to the United States prior to World War II in search of work.

sinigang—a sour broth with vegetables and meat or seafood; one of the few truly authentic Filipino dishes.

Tagalog—a main dialect of the Philippines from which the Filipino language draws many words and expressions.

tinikling—ancient ritual where barefoot performers dance and jump between two clashing bamboo poles on the floor.

utang na loob—means "debt of the inner self" and expresses the moral obligation to repay a gift or favor.

FURTHER READING

Bautista, Veltisezar. *The Filipino Americans (1763–Present): Their History, Culture, and Traditions.* Aurora, Ill.: Bookhaus Publishers, 2002.

Bonus, Rick. *Locating Filipino Americans: Ethnicity and the Cultural Politics of Space.* Philadelphia: Temple University Press, 2000.

Ellis, Kirsten. *Traveler's Companion Philippines.* Old Saybrook, Conn.: The Globe Pequot Press, 1998.

Espiritu, Yen Le. *Filipino American Lives.* Philadelphia: Temple University Press, 1995.

Posadas, Barbara M. *The Filipino Americans* (The New Americans series). Westport, Conn.: Greenwood Press, 1999.

Roces, Alfredo and Grace Roces. *Culture Shock! Philippines.* Portland, Ore.: Graphic Arts Center Publishing Company, 1998.

San Juan, E., Jr. *From Exile to Diaspora: Versions of the Filipino Experience in the United States.* Boulder, Colo.: Westview Press, 1998.

Yuson, Alfred A., ed. *Fil-Am: The Filipino American Experience.* Santa Monica, Calif.: Philippine American Literary House, 1999.

INTERNET RESOURCES

http://www.filipinasmag.com/

The website of the popular print magazine contains articles from the current issue, community news, and Filipino American cooking recipes.

http://www.fanhs-national.org/

The society was organized in 1982 to research and preserve the history of Filipino immigrants in the United States. Its website contains information about the society's archived material and upcoming Filipino American events.

http://www.seattleu.edu/lemlib/web_archives/Filipino/home.html

Compiled by Seattle University's Lemieux Library, this site offers detailed information about virtually every aspect of Filipino American life.

http://www.filipinoamericans.net/

This site provides historical data, traditional recipes, and nationwide directories of Filipino American restaurants, businesses, and stores.

http://pw1.netcom.com/~ntamayo/bookmark.html

A directory of Filipino dance troupes located across the United States and Canada. New links are added regularly.

http://www.filipinoreporter.com/

Founded in 1972, the *Filipino Reporter* is a weekly Filipino American newspaper based in New York. The online edition contains news headlines, sports, entertainment, and featured columnists.

http://islandersbc.50megs.com/

One of the few websites for Filipino Canadians, IslandersBC offers news, business information, and bulletin boards.

http://www.gov.ph/

The official website of the Philippine government. It provides information about tourism, economic issues, and government initiatives.

http://www.seasite.niu.edu/Tagalog/Tagalog_mainpage.htm

Sponsored by Northern Illinois University, this site contains an interactive dictionary that translates Filipino to English and vice versa. There are also listings of popular Filipino phrases, poems, and folk beliefs.

http://www.tayona.com/

This site provides the latest details on important Filipino American issues, and encourages visitors to post their thoughts and feelings on those issues.

http://www.canadianhistory.ca/iv/main.html

This site contains an excellent history of immigration to Canada from the 1800s to the present.

Publisher's Note: The websites listed on this page were active at the time of publication. The publisher is not responsible for websites that have changed their address or discontinued operation since the date of publication. The publisher reviews and updates the websites each time the book is reprinted.

INDEX

Numbers in **bold italic** refer to captions.

INDEX

CONTRIBUTORS

SENATOR EDWARD M. KENNEDY has represented Massachusetts in the United States Senate for more than 40 years. Kennedy serves on the Senate Judiciary Committee, where he is the senior Democrat on the Immigration Subcommittee. He currently is the ranking member on the Health, Education, Labor and Pensions Committee in the Senate, and also serves on the Armed Services Committee, where he is a member of the Senate Arms Control Observer Group. He is also a member of the Congressional Friends of Ireland and a trustee of the John F. Kennedy Center for the Performing Arts in Washington, D.C.

Throughout his career, Kennedy has fought for issues that benefit the citizens of Massachusetts and the nation, including the effort to bring quality health care to every American, education reform, raising the minimum wage, defending the rights of workers and their families, strengthening the civil rights laws, assisting individuals with disabilities, fighting for cleaner water and cleaner air, and protecting and strengthening Social Security and Medicare for senior citizens.

Kennedy is the youngest of nine children of Joseph P. and Rose Fitzgerald Kennedy, and is a graduate of Harvard University and the University of Virginia Law School. His home is in Hyannis Port, Massachusetts, where he lives with his wife, Victoria Reggie Kennedy, and children, Curran and Caroline. He also has three grown children, Kara, Edward Jr., and Patrick, and four grandchildren.

Senior consulting editor STUART ANDERSON served as Executive Associate Commissioner for Policy and Planning and Counselor to the Commissioner at the Immigration and Naturalization Service from August 2001 until January 2003. He spent four and a half years on Capitol Hill on the Senate Immigration Subcommittee, first for Senator Spencer Abraham and then as Staff Director of the subcommittee for Senator Sam Brownback. Prior to that, he was Director of Trade and Immigration Studies at the Cato Institute in Washington, D.C., where he produced reports on the history of immigrants in the military and the role of immigrants in high technology. He currently serves as Executive Director of the National Foundation for American Policy, a nonpartisan public policy research organization focused on trade, immigration, and international relations. He has an M.A. from Georgetown University and a B.A. in Political Science from Drew University. His articles have appeared in such publications as the *Wall Street Journal*, *New York Times*, and *Los Angeles Times*.

MARIAN L. SMITH served as the senior historian of the U.S. Immigration and Naturalization Service (INS) from 1988 to 2003, and is currently the immigration and naturalization historian within the Department of Homeland Security in Washington, D.C. She studies, publishes, and speaks on the history of the immigration agency and is active in the management of official 20th-century immigration records.

PETER HAMMERSCHMIDT is the First Secretary (Financial and Military Affairs) for the Permanent Mission of Canada to the United Nations. Before taking this position, he was a ministerial speechwriter and policy specialist for the Department of National

CONTRIBUTORS

Defence in Ottawa. Prior to joining the public service, he served as the Publications Director for the Canadian Institute of Strategic Studies in Toronto. He has a B.A. (Honours) in Political Studies from Queen's University, and an MScEcon in Strategic Studies from the University of Wales, Aberystwyth. He currently lives in New York, where in his spare time he operates a freelance editing and writing service, Wordschmidt Communications.

Manuscript reviewer ESTHER OLAVARRIA serves as General Counsel to Senator Edward M. Kennedy, ranking Democrat on the U.S. Senate Judiciary Committee, Subcommittee on Immigration. She is Senator Kennedy's primary advisor on immigration, nationality, and refugee legislation and policies. Prior to her current job, she practiced immigration law in Miami, Florida, working at several nonprofit organizations. She cofounded the Florida Immigrant Advocacy Center and served as managing attorney, supervising the direct service work of the organization and assisting in the advocacy work. She also worked at Legal Services of Greater Miami, as the directing attorney of the American Immigration Lawyers Association Pro Bono Project, and at the Haitian Refugee Center, as a staff attorney. She clerked for a Florida state appellate court after graduating from the University of Florida Law School. She was born in Havana, Cuba, and raised in Florida.

Reviewer JANICE V. KAGUYUTAN is Senator Edward M. Kennedy's advisor on immigration, nationality, and refugee legislation and policies. Prior to working on Capitol Hill, Ms. Kaguyutan was a staff attorney at the NOW Legal Defense and Education Fund's Immigrant Women Program. Ms. Kaguyutan has written and trained extensively on the rights of immigrant victims of domestic violence, sexual assault, and human trafficking. Her previous work includes representing battered immigrant women in civil protection order, child support, divorce, and custody hearings, as well as representing immigrants before the Immigration and Naturalization Service on a variety of immigration matters.

JIM CORRIGAN has authored numerous newspaper and magazine articles, as well as several nonfiction books for students. A full-time freelance writer, Corrigan specializes in topics relating to history, travel, and ethnic studies. He is a graduate of Penn State University and currently resides near Harrisburg, Pennsylvania.

Picture Credits

3: Paul A. Souders/Corbis
Chapter Icon: PhotoDisc, Inc.
14: PhotoDisc, Inc.
16: © OTTN Publishing
17: Ariel Skelley/Corbis
18–19: PhotoDisc, Inc.
20: IMS Communications, LLC
25: Hulton/Archive/Getty Images
27: Arte & Immagini srl/Corbis
30: National Archives
32: Hulton/Archive/Getty Images
33: Sandro Tucci/Liaison/Getty Images
34: Melvyn Calderon/Liaison/Getty Images
35: Luis Liwanag/Newsmakers/
    Getty Images
36: Gregorio Cortero/Newsmakers/
    Getty Images
37: IMS Communications, LLC
38: Hulton/Archive/Getty Images
42: Lyndon B. Johnson Presidential
    Library
44: © OTTN Publishing
49: National Archives

54: © OTTN Publishing
56: PhotoDisc, Inc.
58: IMS Communications, LLC
60: © OTTN Publishing
61: PhotoDisc, Inc.
62: Gabriel Mistral/Getty Images
68: Paul A. Souders/Corbis
70: David Greedy/Getty Images
72: Dean Conger/Corbis
75: David Greedy/Getty Images
76: Gabriel Mistral/Getty Images
77: http://www.thealvaradoproject.com
80: Lara Jo Regan/Liaison/
    Getty Images
83: Chris Martinez/Getty Images
84: Justin Sullivan/Getty Images
87: Luis Liwanag/Newsmakers/
    Getty Images
88: Jose Luis Pelaez, Inc./Corbis
92: David Greedy/Getty Images
95: AFP/Corbis
96: Alex Wong/Getty Images

Cover: Michael S. Yamashita/Corbis; **back cover:** Eric Draper/White House/
    Getty Images